THE
BUDDHIST WAY

A Brief Introduction to Buddhism

THE
BUDDHIST WAY

A Brief Introduction to Buddhism

NAGAPRIYA

A dharmachari of the
Triratna Buddhist Order

About the Author

Born in the UK in 1969, Nagapriya studied philosophy at the University of Leeds and later a Masters degree in religions at the University of Manchester. While still an undergraduate, he began practicing with the Triratna Buddhist Community and was ordained as a Dharmachari in 1992. In 2013 he moved to Mexico and helped to found *el Centro Budista de Cuernavaca*, where he is currently Director. He is also co-founder and Director of Editorial Dharmamegha, a publishing company dedicated to sharing Buddhist teachings in the Spanish speaking world. In addition, he is part of a team training men from Latin America for ordination into the Triratna Buddhist Order.

Nagapriya is author of *Exploring Karma and Rebirth* (Windhorse, 2004), *Visions of Mahayana Buddhism* (Windhorse, 2009), and co-author of *AQA GCSE Religious Studies A: Buddhism* (OUP, 2016 with Kevin James) as well as co-author of *AQA GCSE Religious Studies A: Christianity and Buddhism Revision Guide* (OUP, 2018 with Marianne Fleming).

Contents

Introduction:
Pointing towards Buddhism

When we come across a word like 'Buddhism', we think that we should be able to point to what it means, like pointing to an object and saying 'table'. But Buddhism cannot be pointed to so easily. Rather, it gestures towards vast deposits of culture, teachings, and practices that have been laid down over more than 2,500 years. Even the word itself is relatively new; coined in the 19th century to corral a range of spiritual traditions, from many different countries, some of which didn't even know they belonged together. Previously, followers of what we now call Buddhism had simply referred to their spiritual tradition as the Dharma (truth or teaching), or the Buddha-dharma (the teaching of the awakened one) and these terms are still widely used today. Buddhism comes from the word 'Buddha', which refers to someone who has 'woken up' from the sleep of spiritual ignorance, and was a title of respect given to what we would now call the founder of Buddhism: Siddhartha Gautama. There will be more of him later.

Buddhism was born in what is now India. Over the centuries it has spread through most of Asia, interacting with local cultures and taking distinct forms, at times so distinct as to be mutually unrecognizable. Even today upon encountering a wrathful deity from Tantric Buddhism, all flames, fangs, and ferocity, it may seem hard to see what it has in common with the simplicity and tranquility of a zen garden. Yet they do share a common spiritual heritage. So, on what grounds can we decide if a practice, teaching, image or text belongs to Buddhism? There is no simple answer to this, but it has a lot to do with historical development and family resemblances. While the capacity to tell the history of Buddhism is a relatively recent achievement, the resources of modern scholarship allow us to trace its doctrinal, geographical, and cultural development through the ages.

While Buddhism more or less disappeared from India around the 13th century, it had already spread to many parts of Asia, and today continues to flourish there. In a form known as Theravada, Buddhism can be found in many countries to the south such as Sri Lanka, Myanmar, Thailand, Cambodia, Laos, and Vietnam. It also spread to the East, notably China, Tibet, Mongolia, Korea and Japan. Buddhism also flourished in parts of what are now Pakistan, Afghanistan and – in some heady days – reached as far as Iran, also leaving its mark in central Asia and even parts of Russia.

As Buddhism evolved and spread it naturally diversified into different strands or schools. Theravada, whose emblem is surely the clean shaven monk in an orange or yellow robe, has already been mentioned. But distinct forms of Buddhism took root in the Himalayas and Mongolia, known as Tantric Buddhism or Vajrayana, as well as in China and Japan, especially Zen and Pure Land Buddhism. Most of the schools that emerged had their roots in India but took on local colors and customs. Some of the main differences will be sketched out later.

Visibility of Buddhism

Buddhism has become highly visible to the modern gaze. While Buddhists have been quietly going about their practice for many centuries, often totally unaware of fellow Buddhists in other countries, in the 20th and 21st centuries ancient Buddhist traditions have been thrown into sometimes uneasy communication with one another and have become known in many new places. The traumatic Tibetan diaspora of the 1950s, when China took control of the roof the world, catapulted Tantric Buddhism into the consciousness of Europe, the United States, and beyond. Figures like the Dalai Lama became media celebrities. The civil war in Vietnam led to important monks leaving that country and settling elsewhere.

In the 19th century, the only way you could have learnt anything about Buddhism would have been to travel to a traditionally Buddhist country, probably learn a foreign language, perhaps become a monk or nun, and study diligently in the time-honored manner. Today, you can learn about Buddhism through Wikipedia or reading a book like this one and any reasonable-sized town most likely has a Buddhist center or monastery of some kind where you can learn meditation and study Buddhist teachings. Consider me: I was born in England, came across Buddhism in a Yorkshire city called Leeds (more famous for its historic textile industry than for eastern religions), and now live and teach Buddhism in Cuernavaca, Mexico. I had been practicing Buddhism for nearly 10 years before I ever set foot on Asian soil, and even then I visited India to meet new Buddhists inspired by a conversion movement that originated in the 1950s.

Today, if you want to hear the Dalai Lama teach, you don't need to go to Lhasa, you can wait until he visits you or watch a video online. You can find an image of a Buddha in the local gift store and pick up a Buddhist scripture from your local bookshop. You can receive Tantric empowerment in a weekend and learn meditation via an app on your cellphone. But this visibility also comes with a cost or at least with a challenge. So many Buddhist teachings, practices, and cultural forms are available to the present-day seeker, how are you to make sense of it all? Where to start? This short introduction offers some guidelines and marks of reference that should help you to get your bearings and provide a basis to explore further.

Is Buddhism a religion?

Buddhism sits rather awkwardly at the table of religions. In part this is because many defining concepts of religion are derived from Christianity, focusing on a creator God and a holy book – Buddhism has neither of these things. Rather it accommodates many gods (who are often not that important, by the way) and a huge body of scriptures that no one person could ever master. Many people who are attracted to Buddhism prefer not to think of it as a religion at all because for them religion is a bad thing; it can imply control, obedience, repression, even violence. Buddhism usually escapes being tarred with that brush, although it's not without its own shadow. Instead, it is often referred to as a 'philosophy', which sweetens the bitter taste that can be associated with the word religion.

Is Buddhism a philosophy? I studied a degree in philosophy in early adulthood and it was certainly nothing like Buddhism. Most of the time I seemed to be analyzing grammar and studying logic; none of what I learnt had a practical bearing on how to live my life. In fact, it was that disappointment that sent me looking for a Buddhist Center where I could address a deeper, existential longing. We might say that Buddhism, yes, is an applied philosophy, and has something in common with the philosophical traditions of ancient Greece, such as Stoicism and Epicureanism, which didn't just aim to offer abstract analysis but rather a complete programme of spiritual transformation. But in using the word 'philosophy', it would be a mistake to conclude that Buddhism is a purely rational beast. It isn't. Much of the richness of Buddhism lies in its myths, its symbols, its images, and practice is commonly expressed through faith and devotion, though not towards a god.

Some people prefer to think of Buddhism as a *way of life* and it certainly is that, but perhaps even more it is a universe, or even a series of universes. Some of its universes are so spectacular they lift us into an entirely new way of seeing and experiencing, and this is exactly their purpose. It is also common to refer to Buddhism as a *path*. This underlines how Buddhism directs us towards transformation, even towards a goal: enlightenment; liberation from the patterns of thought, speech, and action that cause us and others to suffer. One of the most compact presentations of the Buddhist path is the *Threefold Way*, which consists in the cultivation of ethics, of meditation, and of wisdom. Part 2 of the book introduces this model.

What makes someone a Buddhist?

Buddhists come in many colors, shapes, and sizes. They often believe different things, follow different practices, value different images, wear different clothes, and so on. So, what is it that they actually have in common? How can one Buddhist recognize another, so to speak? This is a complex question because each tradition may have its own definition of what counts as a Buddhist. In the same way that some Christian congregations may not recognize others as truly Christian, some Buddhist schools may not readily see what they share with other Buddhists. For instance, one Buddhist might say that to be a Buddhist is to chant *nam myoho renge kyo* (Homage to the *Lotus Sutra*), another might say it is to practice *zazen* (sitting meditation), and another might say that it is to venerate the monks at the local temple. Each school is likely to identify with its chosen practices and teachings. This is only natural. At the same time, it is possible to recognize shared principles.

A very simple way to define a Buddhist is as someone who *goes for refuge to the Three Jewels*. The phrase going *for refuge* will probably seem a bit strange at first but it is traditionally how Buddhists have expressed their commitment to the Buddhist path. To go for refuge to something means to move towards it, to reverence it, even to value that thing above all else. We might go for refuge to our job or to our hair or even to our washing machine. Buddhists go for refuge to the Three Jewels: the Buddha (the guide and the ideal of enlightenment), the Dharma (the teachings or the truth), and the *sangha* (the spiritual community, especially those with a measure of spiritual insight). We will look more closely at each of the Three Jewels in the following chapters in order to understand how it is that Buddhists go for refuge to each of them. To practice the Buddhist path means to orient oneself towards the Three Jewels on deeper and deeper levels, so that this orientation influences and transforms all aspects of one's life.

While even today most people who identify themselves as Buddhists will have been born into a culture where Buddhism prevails and where their family most likely identifies with Buddhism, perhaps with a small shrine in the home, perhaps regularly giving food to the local monastery, in principle to be a Buddhist expresses an individual commitment not just a cultural affinity. As going for refuge deepens, this commitment becomes clearer and more consistent. At the same time, we should recognize that not all cultures prioritize exclusive religious allegiance. In Japan, for example, it is common for people to venerate not just Buddhism but the indigenous Shinto, and Christianity too, encapsulated in the phrase: 'Born Shinto, marry Christian, die Buddhist'. This kind of multiple identity should alert us to the fact that, at times, the boundaries between religious traditions are not so hard and fast.

Approaching Buddhism

We are likely to come to Buddhism with baggage: with assumptions, expectations, even prejudices. This is unavoidable. According to a traditional analogy, we are likely to arrive as one of three kinds of pot. The first is a pot turned upside down. It cannot retain anything; the precious nectar of the Dharma just flows away, so nothing sinks in. The second kind of pot has a hole in it; slowly but surely everything just leaks away. Finally, there is the poisoned pot, which corrupts everything that it receives.

According to another analogy, when reading or learning about the Dharma we should be like a deer so entranced by the sound of the *veena* (an Indian, lute-like instrument), that it does not even notice the hidden hunter about to shoot his poison arrow.

Listen to the teachings like a deer
listening to music;

Contemplate them like a northern
nomad shearing sheep;

Meditate on them like a dumb person
savoring food;

Practice them like a hungry yak
eating grass;

Reach their result, like the sun coming
out from behind the clouds.[1]

Part 1

THE THREE JEWELS

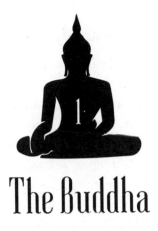

The Buddha

Who is the Buddha?

Images of the Buddha are everywhere: garden ornaments, drinks coasters, key rings, bumper stickers. But who is or was the Buddha and why is his image so significant for Buddhists? The Buddha is the first of the Three Jewels and may be understood on many levels or as having different *bodies* to use a traditional metaphor. First, the Buddha has an earthly body, as expressed through the human being who realized enlightenment and taught the way to others. Second, the Buddha has an archetypal or visionary body as revealed through transcendent Buddhas who became the focus for devotion and even petition. Third, the Buddha has an eternal body, really beyond form, which expresses a spiritual principle intrinsic to reality: the ever-present possibility of spiritual awakening.

The Earthly Body

Usually when we talk about the Buddha (and note that it is *not* Buddha but *the* Buddha) we are referring to a man who lived in ancient India. Unfortunately, ancient India wasn't good with dates and so the Buddha's chronology is much disputed even today and may never be settled with certainty. Scholarly estimates vary wildly from dating the death of the Buddha as early as 544 BCE up to around 370 BCE; a difference of more than 170 years! The recent trend has been towards the later date and many scholars have settled around the year 400 BCE, give or take a few years, as more probable. Given that it is generally accepted that the Buddha lived for 80 years, it is quite likely then that he lived during the great flowering of Greek culture; at the same time as the philosopher Socrates (c.470–399 BCE), the playwrights Sophocles (496–406 BCE) and Euripides (c.480–c.406 BCE), and during the Peloponnesian War between Sparta and Athens (431–401 BCE).

In the earliest scriptural traditions that survive, there is no complete biography of the Buddha although there are texts which record significant moments of his life and teaching career. The earliest full biography is an epic poem written in the first century CE (fully several centuries after the Buddha's death). Indeed, it is hard to speak of a biography in the modern sense because it is clear that the life of the Buddha conforms to a model of Indian saintliness and many of the events that are recounted intend to communicate spiritual teachings rather than record historical facts. They are often symbolic rather than to be taken literally. Of course this doesn't mean that they are not important, just the opposite. Through the narrative of the Buddha's life we can see what early Indian Buddhism considered important with regard to the spiritual path.

The Buddha, whose personal name was Siddhartha Gautama (like in the novel by Hermann Hesse), is generally regarded as having been born in a place called Lumbini, which is in modern day Nepal. At that time what we now call India was made up of many different states and kingdoms. Siddhartha was born into a privileged family of the Shakya clan, which may have been a small republic bordering the foothills of the Himalayas, in what is now northeast India. His father was a clan leader. According to legend, when the Buddha was born he could already walk and talk and when he took his first steps lotuses blossomed to cushion his feet. Siddhartha must have led quite a luxurious life for those days and was married young, at 16. Some biographies speak of him as having a palace for each of the seasons and being entertained by beautiful maidens. He wanted for nothing, it seems. But all was not well.

At the age of 29, Siddhartha is said to have experienced four sights, perhaps better understood as symbolic insights, which served as a turning point in his life. First, he saw a sick man and realized that all human beings are subject to sickness. Second, he saw an old man and realized that he, just like everyone else, was subject to aging. Third, he saw a corpse and it finally dawned on him that he, and all humanity, would die. As a result of these insights, Siddhartha's intoxication with life fell away. There was no going back. He could no longer enjoy his life of luxury as before because he had seen through its limitations. But that wasn't all. Finally, he witnessed a holy man, or *sadhu*, and realized that there was a path or way beyond human frailty and suffering. While the four sights are often presented as having taken place in a single day, or a series of days, they illustrate what was probably a gradual process of disenchantment with mundane life and express the arising of a longing for something transcendent – something that probably we all feel at one time or another. The first three sights in particular express an awareness of the inevitability of suffering, while the fourth suggests the possibility of relief. This preoccupation with the alleviation of suffering was to become a central concern for Buddhism, as we will see later.

The four sights motivated Siddhartha to renounce his privileged life and go forth to live as a wandering ascetic as was common in those days. So he decided to leave his wife and child and, in a dramatic episode, cut off his hair with his sword and handed all his emblems of privilege, including his faithful horse, to his servant. He then plunged into the forest to pursue his 'noble quest' for enlightenment. This search was to last for around six years and, in this time, Siddhartha learnt various meditation practices and spiritual teachings from a series of renunciate teachers. But he was never satisfied with any of them. He also punished himself by following severe ascetic practices such as restricting his food, according to legend surviving on just a grain of rice a day. Obviously he lost a lot of weight and became very weak. Eventually though, Siddhartha realized that his approach to spiritual practice just wasn't working; simply punishing the body was not the means to liberation, so he began to take more solid food and follow a different approach, which he later named the 'middle way'.

Around the age of 35, Siddhartha had his decisive breakthrough. The night of his enlightenment is usually recounted with great drama. It is said that all his doubts, all his spiritual obstacles, appeared before him personified in the figure of Mara, the evil one. Mara sent armies to attack Siddhartha but all their weapons turned to lotus flowers. He then sent his beguiling daughters to tempt Siddhartha but to no avail. Mara even questioned Siddhartha's right to reach enlightenment and, in response, Siddhartha simply touched the earth as witness to his spiritual efforts and realization. For this reason, it is common to see seated statues of the Buddha where he adopts this pose, touching the earth with his right hand.

After his enlightenment, Siddhartha sought out his ascetic companions and began to share the insights that he had been gifted, and so the sangha or spiritual community was born. He came to be known as 'the Buddha', the 'awakened one', as he had woken up from the sleep of spiritual ignorance. After his awakening, and until his death aged around 80, the Buddha lived as a wandering preacher, walking the dusty plains of northeast India in the company of a small group of disciples and staying in more permanent housing only during the rainy season. Wherever he wandered, he gave teachings and begged for alms, as was customary. His followers did the same, although settled monasticism was eventually to become the preferred lifestyle for Buddhist monks. Early Buddhist texts portray the Buddha as a charismatic teacher who welcomes equally rich and poor, high and low. His wisdom is unparalleled, as he regularly defeats rival teachers in debate and displays all kinds of supernormal powers, which arise from his mastery of meditation. This includes performing miracles, such as flying into the air and spouting fire and water, or subduing restless spirits. It is worth noting that the Buddha never wrote down any of his teachings, rather he taught orally. In turn, his teachings were orally passed on for many generations through collective chanting and oral memorization techniques.

It is not clear what impact the Buddha had during his lifetime but in the early scriptures he is depicted as rubbing shoulders with various kings and the well to do, as well as having influential disciples. It is generally accepted that Emperor Ashoka (reigned c.268–232 BCE), who converted to Buddhism after a bloody early reign, played a significant role in the dissemination of Buddhist teachings throughout the subcontinent and beyond.

What is Awakening?

The Buddha is the awakened one, but what exactly is awakening? While it is generally said to be beyond words and beyond explanation, the term 'bodhi' (from which the title Buddha is derived), commonly translated as 'enlightenment', literally means to wake up. According to the Buddha, all beings are beset by three basic spiritual poisons or obstacles: greed, hatred, and delusion. These three poisons cause us to act in ways that cause suffering both to ourselves and others; only through purifying ourselves of these three poisons can we stop causing suffering. Buddhism draws on many metaphors and models to hint at what awakening entails, particularly using light imagery as well as metaphors of freedom and knowledge. Perhaps, in essence, we could see awakening as breaking free from habitual patterns of thought, speech, and conduct that enables a more creative way of living. Awakening is commonly understood as a state of wisdom that enables us to live in a more intelligent way but it is also seen as a condition of compassion in which we recognize our connection to all beings and are inspired to do all that we can to alleviate not just our own suffering but the suffering of others too.

The Archetypal or Visionary Body

After his death, followers of the Buddha continued to transmit his teachings and devotion towards the absent master became a central practice. After all, the Buddha was the teacher, the exemplar, the shower of the way. This devotion came to be expressed in various ways including a practice that recollected the Buddha's spiritual qualities and another that involved visualizing him in the context of meditation.

Even in the earliest Buddhist records, there is the suggestion that the Buddha was more than human – a being apart, beyond the reckoning of the rest of us – that he had a transcendent nature above and beyond time and space, and that he could manifest in different places, at different times, in different bodies. Beliefs emerged that suggested that other Buddhas exist on higher planes or in distant universes and that those with sufficient receptivity and aspiration may enter into communication with them, receive their blessings, and absorb their teachings.

Several centuries after the death of the historical Buddha, texts emerged attesting to some of these transcendent Buddhas, perhaps the most notable of whom is known as Amitabha (Infinite Light), who became a central figure in East Asian Buddhism. Amitabha does not belong to history, but to myth, to the realm of the spiritual imagination. He is composed of pure light, sometimes golden, sometimes the red of the setting sun, and his light shines in all directions. It shines on all beings at all times in all places, blessing them with his wisdom and compassion. According to the scriptures that tell his legend, Amitabha made a compassionate vow infinitely long ago to assemble a perfect world or 'pure land' in which all could be reborn and so attain enlightenment.

He spent five cosmic ages gathering together the materials for this world. The Pure Land that he ultimately assembled is the embodiment of the untold spiritual virtue or merit that he accumulated through all his efforts.

Picture a world where there is no suffering, no negative emotions, where all wishes are granted, a world of scintillating light, of radiant color, and of untold jewels; a world of transcendent beauty and purity, where all beings have golden light bodies. This is a Pure Land – the closest thing to a Buddhist heaven. It is an idyllic realm where conditions for spiritual growth are perfect, free of the hassles and constraints of life as we know it. Here everyone practices the Dharma joyfully and progresses effortlessly towards complete awakening. The only condition required to be born in this ideal realm is that we call to Amitabha with a sincere wish to be reborn there.

The notion of a Pure Land signals a shift away from seeing awakening as something to be strived for through individual effort and towards the idea that Buddhas are reaching out to us, exerting a compassionate influence and drawing us *towards them* through the power of their immense spiritual virtue. The medium of Amitabha's grace is his infinite light; through its influence beings not only feel joy but also begin to act ethically. Thus, his light exerts a transforming impact on those blessed by it. This transforming impact takes place through a transmission of Amitabha's inexhaustible spiritual qualities, known as the transference of merit. Since Amitabha cultivated awakening for many aeons with an altruistic motivation, he has a lot of merit to go around – in fact, an infinite amount. Through his measureless light, this merit is constantly gifted to all beings.

Another of these transcendent Buddhas is called the Medicine Buddha who is often depicted as the color of lapis lazuli – an intensely blue gemstone believed to have healing properties. In his right hand he grasps a healing jar, also made from lapis lazuli, and with his left he sometimes holds a sprig of the myrobalan plant (associated with healing), or else it grows out from his healing jar. The Medicine Buddha radiates an exquisite light of a lapis lazuli hue in all directions, blessing beings not just with good health but with wisdom too. According to scripture, Medicine Buddha made a series of twelve great vows, several of which promise worldly benefits, including restoring those with illnesses or disabilities to health and providing material goods to whoever may need them. Besides this, Medicine Buddha vowed to lead all beings to awakening.[2] Scripture emphasizes the value of reciting the Medicine Buddha's name, or even simply hearing it, promising ethical transformation to those who do so. This, in turn, enables people not only to become generous but eventually even to give life and limb in the service of others.

While this idea of transcendent Buddhas who are reaching out to us may seem a bit remote, even fanciful, it touches on a subtle, spiritual truth: the impulse towards liberation doesn't belong to us, it doesn't belong to the ego. Rather, it is something that irrupts within us, with which we can cooperate, which we can channel. It doesn't seem to belong to our day-to-day reality but breaks in on that reality, like a light shining from an unknown source.

The Eternal Body

In some later currents of thought, the Buddha also came to be understood as the principle of awakening itself, known as Buddha-nature, which refers to the potential that each and every human being has to gain spiritual liberation. It affirms that we can all become Buddhas, and that all human beings have the seed of awakening within them. Some versions of this teaching even suggest that awakening is inherent, that we are somehow *already* Buddhas. Buddha-nature thus highlights the spiritual impulse latent within – that part of us that yearns towards the good, true, and creative – and enshrines this as the defining feature of human experience. In Buddhist scripture, Buddha-nature is illustrated using a series of images, such as gold hidden inside a pit of waste, honey inside a swarm of angry bees, and a golden statue wrapped in dirty rags.[3] The drift of the similes is to emphasize the presence of something exquisitely precious trapped within something foul.

Based on his understanding of Buddha-nature, a Japanese Zen monk called Dōgen (1200–53CE) arrived at a striking insight into the relationship between awakening and the practice of meditation, known as the 'oneness of practice and realization'. For Dōgen, awakening is not a fruit of spiritual practice but rather reveals itself *through* such practice. Instead of conceiving of awakening as a *once and for all* event, it is constantly activated and shared through the discipline of meditation. It becomes neither a possibility in the future nor an achievement of the past but a deeper dimension of the present. Awakening becomes a radical dwelling in the here and now, while practice, rather than being a means to an end, embodies that end.

In some interpretations, Buddha-nature is understood as not just a positive spiritual impulse, but even as the ultimate ground of reality. Thus,

Dōgen asserted that rather than having the Buddha-nature as a potential, 'All beings *are* the Buddha-nature.'[4] Buddha-nature is not a potentiality – or even actuality – within beings, it is the ultimate nature of all things. At the same time, it is nothing apart from the ordinary world: 'the Buddha-nature is a fence, a wall, a tile, a pebble.'[5] Buddha-nature is not transcendental, something other, but is revealed through all experience, no matter how humble or trivial.

Still further, according to Dōgen, awakening to Buddha-nature is not simply a personal event or experience. The activity of the meditator is intertwined with the entire cosmos, all elements of which are engaged in a perpetual process of *reciprocal* awakening, mutually revealing the Buddha-nature for each other.

Devotion and shrines

The Buddha is the central focus of devotion for Buddhists, but he is not God, nor does he represent God. This is often a stumbling block for people from Christian-influenced cultures; there is devotion, there is reverence, but this reverence is not directed towards a creator but rather at a figure who exemplifies the spiritual ideal and who, in some cases, may be seen as capable of helping us towards it. It is not that Buddhism rejected the idea of gods but that the Buddha was seen as far more important. One of the epithets for the Buddha in early tradition was the 'teacher of gods and men'. Early scriptures are littered with episodes where the Buddha gives instruction, not just to a following of monks or lay people, but to spirits of all kinds.

Perhaps curious for us, the Buddha images, which are now so familiar, were not the means by which the Blessed One was memorialized in early Buddhism. Images of the tree under which the Buddha was meditating when he gained enlightenment or a wheel of the dharma were the usual ways to evoke him, as were images of his footprints. An architectural monument, known as a stupa, also became a common symbol for the Buddha and a focus for devotion. A stupa is a kind of tomb or reliquary, some of which are believed to contain the remains of the master. Buddhists would express their devotion towards the Buddha by walking clockwise around a stupa while chanting or meditating: they still do. They may also go on pilgrimage to one of the sites associated with his life, such as Bodh Gaya, where he is said to have gained enlightenment, or Sarnath, where he is said to have first turned the wheel of the Dharma (as the traditional phrase has it).

What is the purpose of devotion in Buddhism?

Through devotional practices that focus on the Buddha, such as bowing, prostrating, chanting, and making offerings, Buddhists cultivate receptivity to his spiritual qualities, even his essence. The Buddha incarnates the spiritual potential that every human has, and so, through expressing devotion towards him, we can connect with that potential and begin to fulfill it within ourselves.

It is customary to make three principal offerings to the Buddha which express both the central importance of generosity, or *dana*, and materialize appreciation of, and receptivity towards, what is spiritually valuable. Within a Buddhist meditation hall or shrine room, the Buddha sits as an honored guest and is commonly presented with candles, which symbolize the light of enlightenment, flowers which symbolize the principle of impermanence, and incense which symbolizes the purity of spiritual life.

Faith or trust is seen as an important spiritual quality within Buddhism as it expresses an intuitive, emotional response to the spiritual ideal. Faith is understood not as trusting in something that can be never known but rather an inspired confidence to fulfill the potential that all human beings have to become like the Buddha. It is joyful, serene, and assured.

The Dharma or Teachings

The second of the Three Jewels is the Dharma, which is usually translated as 'the teachings' or 'the truth'. It also refers to the Buddhist scriptures. Buddhism has a vast body of teachings that have evolved over some 2,500 years and can leave the uninitiated bewildered. How can a teaching be identified as Buddhist and how do all the diverse teachings and traditions fit together?

One way to begin is to go back to the Buddha himself and use some of his basic teachings as a framework to understand later developments, but even the Buddha didn't teach the same thing to everyone, rather he modified his approach to suit the needs of his audience. The Buddha likened his teachings to a raft that is used to cross from the near shore to the far shore. This indicates that his teachings are essentially practical rather than metaphysical. Their purpose is to help beings move towards enlightenment and to reduce their suffering. The Buddha also compared his teachings to a snake, which, if picked up the wrong way, is likely to bite us. This is a warning that understanding the purpose of Buddhist teachings is important if they are to prove helpful rather than harmful.

In one well-known scripture, the Buddha visited a tribe known as the Kalamas. The Kalamas were confused. It seems that many ascetics and spiritual teachers had passed through proclaiming that they alone knew the way, they knew the truth, and that the Kalamas should follow them and no one else. But who to believe? The Kalamas didn't know, so they took the opportunity to ask the Buddha's opinion. His response was quite simple. If a teaching leads to the lessening of ignorance, hatred, and craving, and if is also approved by the wise, then it should be followed. On the other hand, if a teaching intensifies ignorance, hatred, and craving, and is disapproved of by the wise, it should be abandoned. This teaching underlines how the Buddha's approach was practical, not theoretical; he was concerned to help beings to overcome their spiritual limitations which result in suffering.

We have already seen that the Buddha was moved to set out on his path towards awakening when he realized that all of us, without exception, must inevitably suffer. No one is immune from pain and hardship; no matter how carefree, how untroubled we may feel, sooner or later we are going to suffer. Guaranteed. This emphasis on the inevitability of suffering leads some people to think that Buddhism is pessimistic, even life-denying. Surely not *all* life is suffering? This would indeed paint a miserable picture. But the Buddha was not some kind of religious killjoy only able to see misery in everything, however seemingly joyful or life-affirming – far from it. Rather, the emphasis on suffering serves a *practical* purpose – by directing attention towards the imperfections, the ragged edges, and the hardships of human life, Buddhism encourages reflection. It is deliberately one-sided because it aims to inspire us to reach beyond our sufferings to something more fulfilling, more enduring, ultimately awakening or Nirvana.

The Four Noble Truths

This way of thinking is summed up in the formula of the Four Noble Truths, one of the most important of all Buddhist teachings. It is said that the Buddha revealed this contemplation in his very first teaching and it has remained key until today. Exploring it will allow us to gain a better understanding of why Buddhism draws attention to suffering and how Nirvana serves as its antidote. The Four Noble Truths are:

1. Suffering or uneasiness
2. The Cause of Suffering (desire or attachment)
3. The End of Suffering (Nirvana)
4. The Path Leading to the end of Suffering (the Noble Eightfold Path)

The Four Noble Truths function as a kind of reflection programme that we may apply to our lives with the intention to stop heaping up suffering both on ourselves and others.

1 SUFFERING

Buddhism sees human life as shot through with suffering. This is not to say that every aspect of human life is inherently painful or unpleasant, but that suffering is an inevitable dimension of our experience. It goes without saying that there is much beauty, joy, and love in the world, but even in the midst of the wonderful things life brings there is a fly in the ointment. An analysis of suffering in terms of three levels will help to bring this point out better.

First, there is ordinary, basic suffering: pain, loss, death, illness, and so on. This level of suffering is inevitable but we often run away from it, which usually only makes things worse. Second, there is what is known as the suffering of change. While it is clear that we can experience pleasure, this pleasure will come to end sooner or later, which not only causes anxiety but also means that we are likely to experience suffering later on. Third, there is all-pervading suffering or uneasiness. This level of suffering is more subtle, yet more persistent, and hints at the fact that ordinary pleasures and experiences can never fulfill our deepest needs and longings; for this we need a spiritual path.

Equally, life *is* precious and marvelous because it permits us to develop awareness and to move forward on the path towards awakening. The first Noble Truth does not negate life but directs our attention at our discomfort, at the uneasiness we feel deep inside, in order to inspire us to look for something deeper, to live a more significant life. It aims to inspire us to stop investing in limited refuges and to go for refuge to what is truly fulfilling, that is to say the Three Jewels.

2 THE CAUSE OF SUFFERING:

Desire or Attachment

How does suffering arise? It seems to well up from life itself, arriving uninvited and unexpectedly, but according to the Buddha suffering is born from attachment and compulsive desire. If we want something to remain the same, say a relationship, or perhaps our physical body, then we will resist change. But change happens – it can't be avoided. Our lover changes, our body ages, we can't stop it. But our desires may remain the same. When our desires are no longer in harmony with experience, this causes us suffering. Instead of letting go of our desires, our usual response is to hold on tighter, but life slips through our fingers, we can't control it, and this results in suffering.

We are creatures of habit; when we find something we like we become attached to it, whether that be a lover, a car, a vase, or a teddy bear. While we can possess our object of attachment everything is fine: we are blissfully happy. Then what if it is taken away? Our lover leaves us for someone else, our car breaks down, our vase is smashed, or we lose our beloved teddy bear. Depending upon how much of an emotional investment we have made, we may feel upset, bereft, even torn apart.

Our tendency is to see the cause of suffering as being outside of ourselves: in a situation or in another person. So we change our circumstances or we move away from the person thinking that we will be free from suffering, but this isn't what happens because suffering arises from the mind, and this is one of the key Buddhist insights. The poet Milton captures this point when writing about the suffering of Satan after being cast out of heaven:

Horror and doubt distract
His troubled thoughts, and from the
bottom stir
The hell within him; for within him
Hell
He brings, and round about him, nor
from Hell
One step, no more than from Himself,
can fly
By change of place.[6]

An early scripture speaks of two darts of suffering. The first one is physical pain or a shock or a loss. There is nothing we can do about this dart; it pierces us no matter what. However, we then create an active response to this pain, 'Poor me, why me? I don't want to suffer. It's not fair ...' And so on. This is the second dart with which we pierce ourselves with. According to the Buddha, we can learn to stop piercing ourselves with this second dart and so live more freely.

3 THE END OF SUFFERING:

Nirvana

While the term Nirvana refers to a spiritual condition that is supremely positive, its literal meaning of 'quenching' refers to putting out a flame. At first glance, having one's fire put out may not seem so attractive. But according to Buddhist thought, we are all ablaze with greed, hatred, and ignorance, and it is *these* fires that must be dowsed. To become free, we have to stop stoking up the fires that sustain our unhealthy habits. When we do this, we break the unending cycle of birth and death – known as *samsara* – and so put an end to suffering. In positive terms, Nirvana is thus a state of joy, freedom, and understanding.

Nirvana is portrayed in many different ways in early Buddhist scriptures. Because of its lofty nature, it is often spoken of in terms of what it *isn't*, rather than what it *is*. This makes it a bit mysterious. At the same time, Nirvana is also described through images and metaphors, such as the cool cave, the island amidst the floods, the place of bliss, and the refuge.

In early Buddhism, Nirvana was seen as a goal that could be achieved in just one lifetime by following the Buddha's teachings and one who attained Nirvana was known as an *arahant*, literally 'worthy'. In the early scriptures, becoming an arahant seems to be no big deal; dozens of them are listed there. While Nirvana often followed a lengthy period of spiritual practice under the Buddha's guidance, it was sometimes accomplished almost instantly. When an arahant passes away, it is said that they enter Parinirvana (final Nirvana). What this means is not clear, but it seems that they will never be reborn. This has led some to conclude that Nirvana is some kind of ultimate death. According to the Buddha, however, what happens to an arahant after death is beyond reckoning, it is a mystery.

In practice, many Buddhists no longer seek Nirvana in the present life but aim instead to build up spiritual merit through ethical action in the hope of a favorable rebirth in the future. This is especially true of lay people, but may also apply to monks too.

41

4 THE WAY LEADING TO THE END OF SUFFERING:

The Noble Eightfold Path

The way to the end of suffering, to Nirvana, is the Buddhist path. This is described in many different ways but the classic formulation is the Noble Eightfold Path. Its eight elements are:

1. Right View
2. Right Intention
3. Right Speech
4. Right Action
5. Right Livelihood
6. Right Effort
7. Right Awareness
8. Right Meditation

While the elements of the 8-fold path are sometimes regarded as consecutive stages, they may also be seen as dimensions, all of which need to be cultivated as indispensable aspects of any vital spiritual life. Considered as a whole, the 8-fold Path embodies a comprehensive process of self-transformation.

Right view is concerned with developing an outlook that is aligned with the nature of reality and which encourages spiritual development. *Right intention* concerns the motives for practice and purifying our attitude in order to apply the Dharma more wholeheartedly. *Right speech* addresses the area of human communication in the light of the Buddhist ethical precepts. *Right action* concerns the application of Buddhist ethics to our day-to-day decisions. *Right livelihood* also concerns ethics and, more specifically, how we apply the precepts to our working life. *Right effort* concerns how we work on the mind to develop and maintain ethical mental states. *Right awareness* is concerned with the development of mindfulness. Finally, *right meditation* is concerned with the development of super-conscious states of mind and ultimately with seeing into the nature of reality directly.

Buddhist scriptures

The Buddhist scriptural tradition is absolutely vast. Just glancing up from where I am working, I have a whole shelf of Buddhist scriptures, and these only represent a fragment of what exists. There is no equivalent to a Buddhist Bible; instead there is a huge body of material that evolved over many centuries and in many languages. As previously mentioned, the Buddha himself wrote nothing and his teachings were communicated orally for perhaps two or three hundred years. During this time, Buddhism spread and independent communities of followers transmitted the teachings orally. These oral scriptures were gradually committed to writing and, as a consequence, many schools developed their own canons. Much of this material was common but some differed. Most of these early canons have disappeared, while a few survive in fragments.

The largest body of early Buddhist teachings that survives is known as the Pali Canon because it was preserved in a Sanskrit-based language that came to be known as Pali. This Canon is our main source for the Buddha's life and for his key teachings. It consists of three great divisions, or baskets, which reflect the priorities of early Buddhism. The first basket is that of the discourses (*sutta*). In general, this is where many of the Buddha's key teachings can be found. Typically, they are structured in the form of a dialogue between the Buddha and some disciple, or other inquirer. Often the inquirer poses a question and the Buddha answers it. Not all of the discourses follow this model but a great many do. The second great section is the *vinaya*, which means 'discipline' and focuses on the rules that a monk or nun should follow. Finally, the *Abhidhamma*, or 'higher teaching', focuses on the analysis of key aspects of reality, most notably the investigation of various classes of mental states. Such analysis has the aim of helping us to more clearly recognize the states of mind that we dwell in and particularly to determine if these states of mind are afflictive or the opposite. In addition, this process of analysis is concerned to support reflection in relation to the truth that we have no fixed or unchanging nature.

A typical early text is the Meghiya scripture. Here we encounter the Buddha attended by a young novice who has spotted a cool mango grove which he thinks would be perfect for his meditation. Meghiya asks the Buddha if he can be relieved of his duties in order to go and practice meditation. One might think that the Buddha would readily agree but he doesn't. 'Just wait until some other monk arrives to attend to me,' the Buddha says. But Meghiya is not so easily put off and puts up the argument that the Buddha is already awakened while Meghiya still has spiritual work to do and so needs the opportunity to practice intensive meditation. The Buddha still resists, but eventually Meghiya gets his way and goes off to meditate. Almost immediately he is overcome with distractions: sense desire, ill-will, restlessness – all of Meghiya's resistances suddenly float to the surface and he can't meditate at all! Eventually, completely frustrated he returns to the Buddha, rather humiliated by his experience. The Buddha then teaches him five things that help to bring about spiritual maturity: spiritual benefactors, the cultivation of ethics, communication about spiritual practice, mental discipline (especially through meditation), and clarity. The early scriptures are full of little teachings like this and while at first they can seem rather stuffy and repetitive, they repay sustained study.

But the scriptural tradition didn't end with the Pali Canon. Texts continued to emerge for hundreds of years afterwards and some of these showed new characteristics and incorporated new teachings. Most notably, a tradition of visionary literature emerged that was often less focused on doctrine and more concerned with transporting the reader to a spectacular universe, like Dorothy being carried from humdrum Kansas to the magical Oz. No one knows for sure who wrote these scriptures – none of them are individually authored – but most of them developed over time, and are now generally known as *Mahayana sutras*. Mahayana means 'the great way', while 'sutra' means scripture. Mention has already been made of transcendent Buddhas and some of these texts describe their feats and the spiritual universes or *pure lands* in which they live. It is clear that these later scriptures stand on the early teachings and images as their point of departure but everything is taken to a much bigger scale: time periods are incalculable, distances are inconceivable, and everything radiates light and color.

A scripture of this type that remains popular today is the *Lotus Sutra*. This text teaches primarily by means of images and parables. Amongst other things, the *Lotus Sutra* presents the Buddha as beyond time. In one episode, an enormous stupa erupts from the ground to reveal a Buddha, called Abundant Treasures, inside. This Buddha apparently became enlightened an inconceivably long time ago and appears wherever the *Lotus Sutra* is being taught in order to express his approval. When he appears, he makes clear that he has many other bodies in incalculable numbers of other universes and so all of these universes, together with their Buddhas, are revealed to the assembly all at once. Through these mind-blowing images, the text transports us to a dimension that is beyond concepts, beyond space, beyond time, a realm of the spiritual imagination. The purpose of such texts is not so much to impart doctrine as to expand awareness.

Another teaching found in the *Lotus Sutra* is that of Skilful Means which attempts to explain why Buddhist teachings may sometimes appear to contradict one another. A historically informed answer might say it is because they emerged over many centuries and were developed to meet changing spiritual needs, however, in the *Lotus Sutra* an ingenious explanation is offered. The infinite Buddhas create diverse teachings to address the unique needs of beings; to lead each one towards awakening. While on the surface teachings appear different, on a deeper level they serve the same function and are inspired by the same spiritual wisdom.

Skilful means is illustrated by the Parable of the Burning House. There is a rich man who owns a huge, rambling house that has only one exit. The house is falling to bits but even so many people still live in it, including the rich man's many children. A fire breaks out in the house and seeing it the man thinks, 'I know that I can get out with no trouble but my children can't. They are lost in their games, blind to what's happening!'

So he cries out, pointing out the danger that threatens his children and pleads with them to get out of the house before it's too late. But the children are so absorbed in their games they pay no attention. Knowing that time is short, the man thinks of a plan to entice the children out from the house. He tells them that there is a special present waiting for each of them outside the gate: goat-drawn carts, deer-drawn carts, or ox-drawn carts. These gifts probably wouldn't inspire the modern child but it works here – they all come running out and so are saved. But, the father does not give each child the gift as promised; instead he gives all of them the *same* cart, one that is far more precious and spectacular.

This parable intends to show how the Buddha responds to the individual on his or her own terms, presenting the truth in a way that each can understand. Despite the diversity of teachings, ultimately everyone will attain to the same awakening through the Buddha's Skilful Means. In one elegant move, Skilful Means binds all Buddhist teachings into a harmonious unity.

The Sangha or
Spiritual Community

T he third of the Three Jewels is the sangha. This term is taken
to mean different things by different Buddhists. For some, it
refers to the community of monks (and sometimes nuns), for
others it refers to the community of awakened Buddhists, and
for others it refers to the entire body of Buddhist practitioners.
The sangha is the context in which Buddhists follow the path, it can be
a source of inspiration and support, as well as provide the opportunity
for Buddhists to serve others and relinquish the ego-cherishing attitude.

Lifestyles

While perhaps the classic idea of a Buddhist is the neatly shaven monk in his laundered orange robe, this image really just portrays one of many lifestyles through which Buddhists have expressed their commitment over the ages. The earliest sangha was a rather motley crew. At that time, committed spiritual practitioners often renounced village and family life and lived very simply in forests, going from village to village begging for food. They wore discarded rags, were often unkempt, had no fixed abode, and spent a good deal of time alone, meditating. The Buddha himself lived in this way. As his fame spread, he naturally attracted many followers and regular meetings of the sangha emerged. Classically, the sangha would gather on *uposatha* days – the days of the new and full moon – in order to renew connection with the Three Jewels through confession, chanting, and meditation. This tradition continues today.

But the Buddha's sangha was not made up of just renunciates, he attracted many lay followers, among them the influential and well-to-do, but also very humble people. The Buddha numbered within his sangha courtesans, wives of leaders, ex-criminals, all manner of people. Importantly, the Buddha rejected caste and accepted all people into his sangha irrespective of their birth. In fact, he redefined caste in ethical terms: the outcaste is the person who fails to honor the precepts and the correct way to live.

Even in the Buddha's day, people began to donate land and buildings to the sangha, initially for use during the rainy season when it is difficult to travel. This practice of dwelling in one place eventually converted into settled monasticism. The renunciates no longer wandered, but stayed in one place and relied on the local community for support. This lifestyle continues today in some countries, most notably in southern Asia where Theravada is the dominant tradition.

Quite early on, it seems, a distinction emerged between the renunciate sangha and people living a more family-based or lay lifestyle. Little by little, these two groups began to fulfill different roles and expectations. The job of the monks or nuns was to live the spiritual life, follow the monastic rules, including celibacy, teach the lay people the Dharma, and strive towards enlightenment. In turn, the role of the lay people was to be devout, observe special days and festivals, and, above all, support the monastic sangha by giving food, clothing, and other material necessities. In doing so they accumulated a kind of spiritual capital, known as merit, which would benefit them when reborn, perhaps enabling them to practice the Dharma more intensively next time around. Effectively, this meant that lay people came to live the spiritual life vicariously through the monastic sangha.

Buddhist monasticism was transmitted to all countries where Buddhism found a foothold. In Tibet, for instance, vast monastic complexes emerged, like small towns, where sometimes thousands of monks lived in a kind of monastic university. It became common for families to send one of their sons to become a monk, sometimes for financial reasons, sometimes for spiritual ones. This tradition was only disrupted when China invaded Tibet in the 1950s forcing important lamas to flee and so opening up the treasures of Tibetan Buddhism for the world.

Monasticism spread to China, Korea and Japan too. Particularly in China, monasteries developed into a kind of hacienda in which monks and lay people produced various goods, including crops, and traded them to pay the monastery's expenses.

The Ideal Buddhist

In one early text, the Buddha declares that just as there are many amazing types of creature in the ocean, so in his sangha are there many amazing types of beings. For early Buddhism, the ideal Buddhist, or the ideal towards which all Buddhists aspired, was the arahant. The arahant is the Buddhist saint who has broken free of all spiritual obstacles, is free, wise, peaceful, and content. He, or she, has attained Nirvana and so has reached the spiritual goal. This should be good enough for anyone you might think but apparently it wasn't.

In some later scriptures, which promoted the Mahayana (Great Way), the arahant ideal came to be seen as rather limited, inward-looking, and lacking in compassion. After all, the aim of the arahant was to be free from the cycle of birth and death. Mahayana texts taught the bodhisattva ideal as the universal path. The bodhisattva (or enlightenment being) aims to reach awakening not just for him or herself but also for the sake of all beings. The bodhisattva does not seek to escape from the world of suffering but, instead, deliberately chooses to re-enter this world in order to help other beings reach freedom. The bodhisattva ideal becomes a cosmic vision in which the ultimate goal is the awakening of all beings. For the bodhisattva, the key moment in his or her path is the arising of the *bodhichitta*, or the will towards awakening. This is a compassionate urge to live out the spiritual ideal for altruistic reasons, that is to say, not just to achieve personal peace or liberation but to serve the spiritual needs of the whole universe. While this ideal was clearly seen as a realistic aspiration in some of its presentations, it also came to be associated with transcendent bodhisattvas, beyond space and time, who are working to help all beings towards enlightenment and with whom the devout may enter into communication.

One of the most notable, and perhaps striking of these transcendent bodhisattvas, is known as Avalokiteshvara (the Lord who looks down), who is especially associated with compassion. In one of his forms, Avalokiteshvara has 11 heads and a thousand arms. According to legend, Avalokiteshvara contemplated all the suffering in the world and was overcome by his inability to relieve it. His body broke into a thousand fragments and his head into 10 pieces. The Buddha Amitabha then put Avalokiteshvara back to together, this time with a thousand arms, which could reach out in all directions and respond to the needs of beings, and with 11 heads (including his own), in order to be able to see what each being needs to become free from suffering.

Diversity of schools

1. Theravada
2. Tibetan Buddhism
3. Zen
4. Pure Land Buddhism

THERAVADA

Several mentions have already been made of Theravada ('doctrine of the elders'), which is the sole surviving school of ancient Indian Buddhism. Theravada strongly emphasizes the separate spiritual roles of monks and laity. The monks and nuns are the religious professionals, they do not work, but rather depend on the laity for their material needs; they are celibate and committed to having few possessions. This reflects a general concern with renunciation as a key means to liberate ourselves from desire and attachment. In addition, the role of the monks and nuns is to instruct the laity on principles of Dharma. The laity, on the other hand, serve the monks as their primary spiritual practice in the belief that this will benefit their future rebirth.

Most of the basic Buddhist teachings can be found in Theravada: the Four Noble Truths, Dependent Arising, the five ethical precepts, and the three marks of existence, to name just a few examples. Theravada is truly a treasure trove of Buddhist riches. It is generally regarded as a conservative tradition; after all, it has successfully conserved the Pali Canon for some 2,000 years or more! We might say that the teachings found in Theravada Buddhism form the foundations of Buddhism. Even where later schools diverged and developed new ideas and practices, it is almost always possible to trace the innovations back to basic teachings.

TIBETAN BUDDHISM

Tibetan Buddhism has perhaps become the most visible and photogenic face of Buddhism in the contemporary world, which is quite remarkable for a country that has a population of a similar size to Denmark. Tibetan Buddhism follows an approach known as *vajrayana* (Diamond Path), which combines Mahayana philosophy with complex ritual, a wide array of deities, and even shamanic practices. While its approach originated in India, it achieved its classic form in Tibet, Bhutan, and Mongolia, even reaching parts of Russia.

The most notable representative of Tibetan Buddhism is of course the Dalai Lama who traditionally functioned not only as the spiritual inspiration for all Tibet, but also as its political leader (now in exile). The Dalai Lama and other important teachers, known as *tulkus*, are believed to be bodhisattvas who have chosen to be reborn in the world of suffering to lead others towards spiritual freedom. Some of these teachers have been 'rediscovered' again and again throughout the centuries and their rebirths have taken up important spiritual roles.

Tibetan Buddhism is an extremely rich, complex, even bewildering tradition, not at all easy to grasp without dedicated study, in part because it synthesizes many different influences. Perhaps one of its most striking features is its focus on wrathful deities. One such figure is known as Yamantaka (Destroyer of Death) who, in one of his manifestations, has no less than 34 arms and 16 legs. His principal head – he has nine in all – is a bull with long black horns and his body is blue-black with a big hanging belly. He has fangs, a lolling tongue, and large red lips. His eyes bulge with rage. He is engulfed in flames and crushes animals and humans underfoot. Such terrifying figures can seem more like demons than enlightened beings, drinking blood from a skull cup, wielding knives and other weapons. They are full of energy and power; it seems a far cry from the tranquility and peace of a meditating monk. Yet, these esoteric figures are bodhisattvas or even Buddhas, dedicated to helping all beings to overcome their spiritual obstacles. They take a wrathful form because this energy is sometimes what is needed to break through spiritual obstacles and to destroy the power of greed, hatred, and delusion.

The ritual service of deities is a key practice within Tibetan Buddhism. Through visualizing, chanting, and making offerings to a Buddha or bodhisattva, the devout Tibetan aims to become a channel for the blessing of this figure and even for his compassionate influence in the world.

Tibetan Buddhism also places much emphasis on death and preparation for death. Indeed, it developed a whole technology of death-related practices, perhaps the most widely known of which is embodied in what has become known as the *Tibetan Book of the Dead*. Essentially, this book offers guidance as to how to die well and use the death process as an opportunity to gain enlightenment. It is one of a number of texts unique to Tibetan Buddhism, which are called *termas* (hidden treasures). Termas are secret texts or objects that have supposedly been hidden by an enlightened master to be discovered at a later, more auspicious time; they may be hidden in a cave or even inside someone's mind.

Termas form part of the Tantras, which is a body of esoteric texts not for general consumption but rather to be used by a guru to train his advanced disciples. While you can now read Tantras on the Internet, in principle they constitute a secret knowledge, to be transmitted only to the properly prepared. The Tantras are difficult to understand and interpret because they use highly symbolic language. For instance, while Tantric sex instantly piques much interest, the union that it expresses is most commonly understood to symbolize the overcoming of opposites, and the fusion of wisdom and compassion.

Some strands of Tibetan Buddhism emphasize what is called *attitude training* (*lojong*). Within this approach, there is a teaching known as the four preliminary reflections or the four mind turning reflections, which is said to inspire renunciation of mundane life and going for refuge to the Three Jewels. The first reflection is that we have been gifted the precious human birth. We have a human body, the capacity to reason, we live in a time and place where we are free to practice the Dharma, where we have the opportunity and where the teachings are freely available. We should seize this precious chance before it slips away. Second, we reflect on impermanence, that we will die, and that all will die, which inspires us with a sense of urgency to make the most of the opportunity for spiritual awakening that life offers us. Third, we reflect on the results of our actions and see that if we don't live according to ethical principles, we will suffer both in this life and perhaps in future lives. Finally, we reflect on the limitations of samsara or the unenlightened mind, how it traps us in suffering, how it seems like a merry-go-round that we just can't get off. All these reflections inspire a withdrawal from mundane goals and concerns and a wholehearted desire to go for refuge to the Three Jewels.

ZEN

Whenever we see something elegant, austere yet beautiful, we may be tempted to say, 'Ooh, that's so Zen.' Zen seems to suggest something quite ordinary, which also reveals something extraordinary, like an epiphany. The haiku of Bashō (1644–94) illustrates this:

> *On a bare branch*
> *A rook roosts:*
> *Autumn dusk.*[7]

Zen first emerged in China from around the 7th century (where it was known as Chan) and spread to Korea, Vietnam and Japan. While it draws strongly on Mahayana teachings, Zen expresses these teachings by means of various artistic disciplines, including poetry, ink drawing, martial arts, and even through tea. Amongst other things, it developed a unique literature known as encounter dialogue, which records the supposed meetings in which the master awakens his disciple – or sometimes just baffles him – through striking him a blow, through a shout, gesture or offbeat comment. For example, a monk asked Yunmen: 'What is the Buddha?' Yunmen answered: 'A dried shit-stick.'8

Encounter dialogue, such as recorded in the *Blue Cliff Record* or *Gateless Gate*, replaces the individual cultivation of awakening with the transformative encounter that may occur between master and student. The Zen master catches the student napping, frustrates him, even turns him upside down, in order to shatter the habitual mind. Through his contact with the master, the student's awakened nature is activated, even rediscovered. The *kōan* later built on this idea by substituting the intensive contemplation of a 'critical phrase' spoken by a past master for live encounter.

The critical phrase serves to spark awareness of the student's intrinsic Buddha-nature. This occurs by provoking confusion, which builds into a great ball of doubt. This 'great doubt' results from the student's incapacity to solve the kōan conceptually and becomes so intense that the student may feel as though he or she were gnawing on an iron bar. In time, the doubt fuses with the critical phrase and the mind eventually becomes trapped in a state of perfect concentration. When the ball of doubt explodes, self-referential habits dissolve away and the innate clarity of the mind is restored.

Classically, Zen is associated with the practice of meditation but it is worth noting that at least some Zen masters have actually been suspicious of meditation, at least when pursued in the belief that it might bring about awakening. At first this may seem a bit confusing. In one well-known story, Master Huairang (677–744) challenges his student Mazu (709–88) as to why he spends so much time meditating. Mazu replies that he meditates in order to move closer to enlightenment. Huairang then picks up a piece of tile and begins grinding it on a rock.

Confused, Mazu asks, 'Master, but what are you doing?' Huairang replies, 'I'm grinding this into a mirror.' 'But that's ridiculous,' says Mazu, 'how you can you make a mirror by grinding a piece of tile?' Huairang retorts sharply, 'Well, how can you possibly become a Buddha by sitting in meditation?'.

This story is not meant as a rejection of meditation as a whole but challenges the idea that enlightenment can be achieved through effort. In this teaching, enlightenment cannot be cultivated because it is the true nature of the human mind and so ever present by way of Buddha-nature. To see into one's own nature is to realize that one is already a Buddha, that one is inherently awakened.

In Japan, Zen is divided into two main schools. The first, Rinzai, emphasizes the study of kōans while the second, Soto, emphasises the single practice of sitting meditation or zazen. Soto is characterized by strict discipline and an austere but exquisite minimalism — its signature image is perhaps black-robed monks sitting in zazen, eyes half-open, facing the wall to avoid distraction. In recent decades, both traditions have been active in spreading Zen around the world, especially in the USA.

PURE LAND BUDDHISM

Pure Land Buddhism centers on the transcendent Buddha, Amitabha (Amida in Japan), who has already been mentioned, and at first glance might easily be mistaken for a kind of theism. Strange to say, at least in structure, Pure Land thought and practice offer some striking parallels with Lutheran theology. Devotion to Amitabha originated in India but grew in China and consolidated in Japan into several distinct schools, which remain important even today.

Whereas in the classic Buddhist model enlightenment is attained through strenuous individual effort, perhaps even over many lifetimes, according to the Pure Land perspective human beings are really incapable of lifting themselves out of ignorance, and the sooner they realize this the better. This will allow them to entrust themselves to Other Power. Other Power refers to the vows that Amitabha made infinitely long ago to create a Pure Land in which those who sincerely call to him may be reborn and so attain enlightenment. Entrusting to Other Power means to give up the idea that we can become enlightened through our own spiritual efforts and instead become receptive to the spiritual blessing and influence of Amitabha, to recognize that Amitabha is constantly gifting the immense merit of his incalculable spiritual virtue to us while expecting nothing in return.

The Japanese master Shinran (1173–1263) is arguably the most important figure in Pure Land thought and practice. Ordained as a monk at a young age, in his late twenties Shinran came to feel that he had made absolutely no spiritual progress, despite his best efforts over many years. After a crippling spiritual crisis, Shinran came to believe that the only practice of value is the *nembutsu*, which is the recitation of the mantra *namo amida butsu* (Homage to Amida Buddha). In accordance with Amitabha's vow, the nembutsu is the means by which those who wish to be born in his land can call on Amitabha. However, for Shinran, one does not recite the nembutsu in order to be born in Amitabha's Pure Land, but rather out of gratitude for the fact that Amitabha has already assured such rebirth.

Shinran came to emphasize a transformative moment or attitude known as *shinjin*, which is sometimes translated as true entrusting or even faith. Through *shinjin*, the practitioner gains confidence that his or her rebirth in the Pure Land is assured, and that their mind is fused with that of Amitabha, even while he or she remains a flawed, foolish being. Practice does not earn enlightenment but expresses gratitude towards Amitabha for having gifted his mind and merits to all beings. *Shinjin* itself is understood as a gift from Amitabha, rather than something to be cultivated.

This approach seems deceptively simple: all we need to do is have confidence that Amitabha has guaranteed our future enlightenment, and even this confidence has been gifted to us. How easy is that? But what if we don't have that confidence? This seems to create a kind of paradox: we don't have *shinjin* but equally we can do nothing to cultivate it. While the Pure Land perspective can at first seem almost like the opposite of Buddhism, and even a recipe for spiritual laziness, the adoption of Other Power can be understood as the renunciation of the ego-centric attitude in order to enable a more compassionate volition to work through us. The primary obstacle to our enlightenment is our own self-obsession; once we give up the idea that we have the capacity to release ourselves from suffering, the possibility of opening ourselves to a will that seems to come from beyond us arises. The fact that the spiritual impulse is seemingly gifted to us instead of generated from within helps to offset the danger of spiritual superiority or pride and, instead, inspires a humble gratitude in which the practitioner continues to recognize his or failings while feeling miraculously blessed by Amitabha's compassionate light.

Buddhist Festivals

We have already seen how gatherings of the sangha have served to strengthen confidence, develop fellowship and clarify and deepen the practice of going for refuge. Many Buddhist festivals are celebrated across the world but one of the most important is Buddha Day (sometimes called Wesak), which celebrates the Buddha's enlightenment, usually on the full moon of May. Then there is Dharma Day, which celebrates the fact that the Buddha chose to teach the Dharma and is usually celebrated on the full moon of July. Sangha Day, held on the full moon of November, celebrates the fellowship of spiritual community. Another important festival is Parinirvana Day, usually in February, which commemorates the death of the Buddha. There are also many regional festivals and celebrations dedicated to particular deities or teachers.

Part 2

THE THREEFOLD WAY

Ethics

The Threefold Way begins with ethics but this shouldn't fool us into thinking that Buddhist ethics is simply a basic or preliminary practice. Indeed, ethics may be understood as the whole of the spiritual path because it involves the transformation of every aspect of our lives in the light of the Buddhist vision of existence. Ethics in Buddhism is not a matter of rule-following, not a matter of behaving well in order to receive a reward or to avoid a punishment, nor is it a matter of obedience, rather it is a question of developing a tender conscience, a conscience that is sensitive to the ways in which human beings are capable of hurting one another as well as helping one another. Buddhist ethics is about developing a kind of spiritual sensitivity to oneself and others, which involves the purification of mental states and a refinement of behavior. In this chapter we will look at a simple model of Buddhist ethics known as the five precepts. Before doing so, however, it will be helpful to sketch out the principles that underpin the Buddhist approach to ethics, notably the primary importance of mind and the notion of karma.

Karma and Rebirth

Buddhist ethics rests on the principle of karma, which is summed up beautifully in the following passage from an early Buddhist text:

Experiences are preceded by mind,
led by mind, and produced by mind.
If one speaks or acts with an impure
mind, suffering follows even as the
cart-wheel follows the hoof of the ox
(drawing the cart).

Experiences are preceded by mind, led
by mind, and produced by mind. If
one speaks or acts with a pure mind,
happiness follows like a shadow that
never departs.

The Dhammapada[9]

While it is one of the most widely known Buddhist terms, karma is also one of the most misunderstood. It is not fate or destiny, nor is it a principle of just desserts, it simply means 'action' and governs how our behavior shapes both the kind of person we are and the world that we experience. Key to this is individual intention or will. The term karma can be used in three main ways. First, it refers to an ethical principle that governs human conduct – not just physical actions but speech and thoughts too. Second, a karma is simply an intentional act (where action can include speech and thought). Third, karma as popularly used refers to the accumulated conduct (good or bad) of the individual – like 'Winston Churchill's karma' – and the potential consequences of this.

Traditional Buddhism interprets karma in cosmological terms, as governing the rebirths of all beings. In particular, it determines what category of being they will be reborn as; if we act especially badly, we cannot expect a human rebirth next time around. According to one traditional model, there are six main types of rebirth: as a god, as a Titan (a kind of angry god), as a hungry ghost, as a tormented soul, as an animal, or as a human being. The kind of world and body that a being will be reborn into depends upon how he or she acts in their previous life (their karma). While it may seem that the god realm would be our favored option, the human realm is said to be the most conducive for making progress towards enlightenment. In this realm, there is a measure of suffering which may encourage beings to look for something transcendent but, at the same time, there is also pleasure which means that they are not simply drowning in their sorrows, unable to act creatively.

Understood more psychologically, karma determines the kinds of habits we develop, it colors our experience of the world. In turn, this influences how others behave towards us. The six realms described above can also be understood as psychological states. When driven by the unhealthy impulses of greed, hatred, and delusion, karma is *unskilful*. When inspired by their positive counterparts of generosity, love, and understanding, karma is *skilful*. Skilful karma creates merit, a kind of spiritual bank deposit that leads to positive outcomes both in this life and beyond; it basically leads to happiness, ease, and satisfaction. Unskilful karma, on the other hand, leads to suffering but not as a punishment, it is simply the natural outcome. Buddhist ethics is about cultivating skilful mental states and expressing them through skilful actions. Such actions establish the basis for happiness in the future and even a favorable rebirth. They also bring about a process of purification, which enables the possibility of rising into higher states of consciousness, and the realization of enlightenment. Skilful action models the conduct of a Buddha.

Karma is not some neat principle of cosmic justice. If we do one bad thing, we shouldn't necessarily fear immediate, cosmic vengeance, like being struck by lightning or our house being carried away in a freak tornado. Instead, karma usually works on the basis of *repetition*. Through doing something again and again, we create a habit. This habit imprints itself into the pattern of our lives. We could liken it to the principle of momentum; once we have got a habit well established it is difficult to break. It is not exactly that the world punishes or rewards us for our actions but rather we create a whole world for ourselves that reflects our choices and intentions. Nobody enjoys being around a selfish or hateful person whereas everyone enjoys the company of someone kind and generous. If we want to know whether we are living a skilful life, all we need to do is look around and see the quality of our relationships with others.

Karma is sometimes used to explain *everything* that happens in life – good or bad – as though the universe were a moral feedback loop.

But karma is only a specific instance of the general Buddhist principle of conditionality or dependent origination. There are many factors that influence our lives besides karma. For example, if I go out for a walk and it starts raining, this is not a result of bad karma. It's just bad weather and the factors that influence the weather do not include my degree of moral purity; it rains on the Dalai Lama just as it does on the common criminal. But *how* we respond to the weather will reveal our karmic tendencies. While karma says that our bad conduct leads to suffering, it doesn't mean that when something bad happens to us, this *must* be a fruit of our karma. Victims of disasters such as earthquakes or plane crashes, for instance, are not directly reaping the consequences of their past bad behavior, they simply live in a world where beings are subject to such tragedies.

The Five Ethical Precepts

A simple model of Buddhist ethics is expressed in the five ethical precepts found in early Buddhism. These precepts offer a template for how a more awakened person might live and in modeling this conduct Buddhists move closer to living like the Buddha.

1. I undertake to refrain from harming living beings (compassion)
2. I undertake to refrain from taking what has not been freely given (generosity)
3. I undertake to refrain from harming others through sexual activity (stillness, simplicity, and contentment)
4. I undertake to abstain from false speech (truthfulness)
5. I undertake to abstain from intoxicants that cloud the mind (mindfulness)

In its basic form, each precept is concerned with stopping doing something harmful, however, at a more advanced level it involves the conscious and patient cultivation of its opposite. In this sense it is not a question of just ticking off the precepts and then concluding that one is now morally pure; rather, cultivating the spiritual qualities that the five precepts embody is understood to be a lifetime's work, even the work of many lifetimes! The precepts may be practiced at increasingly subtle and refined levels, most especially at the level of the mind.

THE FIRST PRECEPT: NONVIOLENCE OR COMPASSION

It is well known that Buddhism promotes nonviolence but this doesn't just mean refusing to fight in wars or not killing people. Violence is an attitude that underlies many of the things that we do and rests on a relationship of power with others instead of a relationship of love, respect, and even compassion. Power is so endemic to our ways of relating both to ourselves and others that much of the time we don't even notice it but as our conscience becomes more refined and sensitive we may begin to see the subtle ways we exert power or succumb to power. For instance, we may notice how we impose upon or manipulate others in order to get what we want.

One of the obvious ways in which Buddhists express their commitment to the first precept is through becoming vegetarians or even vegans. At the same time, it is just one way to express care and sensibility to other beings on the planet and there is much more to the principle of compassion than simply not killing them. Cruelty, or a fault of compassion, may show itself in many ways both direct and indirect. For instance, while we may not wish suffering on others, we may live a lifestyle that indirectly causes them suffering.

A further way that the first precept may be practiced is in relation to care for the environment and the planet. Rather than seeing the Earth as a pile of resources to be used, the first precept encourages us to take care of the Earth to ensure its health and wellbeing. This is likely to involve reducing our impact on the planet, our carbon footprint, for instance, and making use of renewable resources.

The first precept does not necessarily imply that a Buddhist will never use force, for instance in self-defense, but rather that this force will not express hatred. There may be circumstances in which using force to protect or defend someone may express a compassionate response. At the same time, it is noteworthy that Buddhist leaders, such the Dalai Lama or Thich Nhat Hanh, have generally encouraged nonviolent protests, even in response to intolerable situations.

A further theme that falls within this precept is abortion. Owing to beliefs in rebirth, Buddhism generally sees life as beginning at conception and that consequently abortion involves taking life. There may be circumstances, however, where abortion is seen as the lesser of two harms, such as when the mother's life is at risk. This and many other ethical issues are often complex and sometimes there may be no easy answer. Every decision has consequences but in principle a Buddhist aims to act from a basis of compassion in reaching their decision.

THE SECOND PRECEPT: GENEROSITY

Generosity (or dana) may be regarded as the most basic of Buddhist practices because it works directly on the most fundamental obstacles to spiritual liberation, which are selfishness, greed, and attachment. Giving is a means to weaken self-obsession and to open out towards other beings, to recognize the value of their needs and happiness.

In traditional forms of Buddhism, the laity is encouraged to give to the monks and nuns. These gifts typically include food, clothing, and other basic needs. It is common to make donations for the upkeep of monasteries or temples. It is also customary to make offerings to the Buddha or to shrines that honor other enlightened beings. According to a traditional list there are six ways in which giving may be practiced. First, and most obviously, we may give material things; food, shelter, clothing, and so on. Second, we may give confidence or fearlessness – this may seem a somewhat surprising gift but it is widely emphasized in traditional Buddhism. Third, we give education and culture. Fourth, life and limb – without condoning martyrdom, Buddhism nevertheless allows for circumstances in which we may prioritize the needs of others over our own, even at cost to ourselves. This is not as some kind of self-punishment, rather as an expression of compassion. Fifth, we may give merit – many Buddhist practices and ceremonies rest on the idea that if we gain benefits from spiritual practice it is good to share these with others. Finally, and perhaps most important of all, we may give the Dharma.

Giving expresses the principle of renunciation, the letting go of attachment, which brings freedom and happiness. Instead of always thinking in terms of one's own benefit or quid pro quo, generosity involves giving without expectation of reciprocity and without calculation. We are so accustomed to contractual relationships with other people that giving (or even receiving) seems to go against the grain. If someone gives us something we usually wonder what they want from us.

We often resist giving because we feel that we will have less and be less happy if we do so. This touches on a fundamental delusion that happiness can be achieved by possessing things. It is obviously not true and yet it is so easy to get seduced by this kind of logic, especially in societies that see consumption as the route to happiness. This resistance to giving or letting go also expresses a lack of abundance and a lack imagination. If awareness is directed not towards what we lack or what we desire but instead towards all of the opportunities and possibilities we are blessed with, instead of feeling impoverished, we can begin to see that we are rich in so many ways. This may lead to a feeling of gratitude, which connects us more fully to others and may inspire generosity as an expression of that gratitude.

THE THIRD PRECEPT: STILLNESS, SIMPLICITY AND CONTENTMENT

While in its basic form, the third precept is concerned with not causing harm to others through sexual activity; it really touches on the whole area of desire. According to Buddhism, compulsive desire is the root cause of much of our suffering, and also one of the main reasons why we make others suffer. Thus, letting go of such desire is key to developing contentment and living more harmoniously with others. This doesn't mean that all desire is bad and should be got rid of but in part involves recognizing that true happiness is not found simply by indulging unfettered desire. Desire can express a kind of addictive tendency, which can never be satisfied. We overload our objects of desire with what are sometimes complex needs. Moreover, our desire often blinds us to the needs of others, which means that we cause them harm often without even realizing it.

In relation to sex, Buddhist ethics does not privilege one kind of relationship above another; heterosexuality, for instance, is not seen as more ethical than homosexuality. Having one sexual partner is not more ethical than having several; what is at issue is whether we cause harm to others through our sexual activity. This can be owing to a lack of care, perhaps through using others as objects of gratification, or through control and manipulation. Sex is such a powerful impulse that it very readily drives us to act from selfish motives.

In the monastic sangha, of course, celibacy has always been the favored model, in part because of the obligations and complications that family life can sometimes bring. Equally, the vast majority of Buddhists are not celibate and so this remains a key area of ethical practice.

THE FOURTH PRECEPT: TRUTHFULNESS

While at its most basic level, the fourth precept encourages telling the truth, it really addresses the whole arena of human communication. According to one traditional source, the Buddha once said that our tongues are axes with which we cut down the tree of our virtue. It is so easy to cause damage through speech; one careless comment may result in hurt that may last for years. Speech should not only be truthful but also kind, helpful, and harmonious. There is a useful checklist found in an early Buddhist scripture about how we can tell if we should say something or not. In advice to Prince Abhaya, the Buddha offers six criteria: is it true or false, is it of benefit or is it harmful, is it agreeable or disagreeable? It is never appropriate to communicate something that is untrue, even if it is agreeable. Equally, something may be true and yet it may not be beneficial to communicate it. Finally, something may be disagreeable yet true and of benefit and therefore still worth saying. So, it may sometimes be appropriate to say things that are difficult to hear, however, especially in such situations, the Buddha underlines how it is also important to pick the right moment to communicate.

Many of us talk a lot but what we say is not always useful, either for ourselves or indeed for anyone else. In general, the Buddhist tradition places a lot of emphasis on reducing our level of talking and focuses on silence. While it might seem that silence impedes communication, it is often the opposite: silence can permit richer communication beyond the chatter of words, which may distract us from arriving at a deeper human encounter.

THE FIFTH PRECEPT: CLARITY OF MIND

The fifth precept underlines the importance of mind and mental states in the refinement of ethics. While at its most basic level it is about reducing and even abandoning activities that cloud the mind, at higher levels it involves positively cultivating clarity and awareness, which in turn permits enhanced ethical sensitivity. It is fairly obvious that alcohol and drugs impair awareness and reduce our capacity to think clearly and act with good judgment, but there are many other ways in which we fill the mind with junk and so reduce our capacity to respond to life creatively. Consider the amount of time spent grazing the Internet, collecting useless facts that – even while we forget them almost immediately – overload the mind with unnecessary information which reduces clarity and tranquility. The mind is bombarded all day with images and information, especially in cities, and even while we ignore it this information is still cluttering the mind.

The fifth precept indicates the importance of being selective about what input we expose the mind to or, in a traditional phrase, 'guarding the gates of the senses.' One text describes the mind as a kind of wound that we must protect to avoid it becoming infected. Constantly exposing the mind to objects that provoke desire is one of the ways that we may aggravate the wound and intensify our own suffering. Even just being busy can be a way of clouding the mind, avoiding what is of real importance, or failing to notice the needs of a friend. At times, it is uncomfortable to face deeper truths and it can seem easier to distract ourselves instead but at the cost of superficiality.

The fifth precept also hints at the inner work required to live in a state of clarity and contentment. While it is clearly important to take care in relation to external stimulus, much of what clouds the mind is the internal chatter that seems to never switch off. Repetitive thoughts, negative judgments about ourselves and others, regrets, obsessive desires or fears, all of this mental noise impairs clarity and prevents contentment. Slowing down, doing nothing, and practicing meditation are some of the ways to move towards stillness and contentment.

Purification: confession, apology, and forgiveness

Buddhism makes widespread use of the metaphor of purification. Through their ethical conduct, beings become purified which enables them to live in a way that harmonizes with reality. One of the key tools in the process of purification is confession. While, for many people, confession immediately conjures up ideas of Catholic Church and Hail Marys, in Buddhism it does not have the aim of absolution. Rather it is a practice that enables Buddhists to more fully understand the ethical quality of their actions, their impact on themselves and others, and to cultivate more skilful conduct in the future through developing a more tender conscience. When appropriate, confession may also lead to apology. Forgiveness of a wrong done is also important because this involves letting go of resentment or even hatred towards someone who may have harmed us.

The Ethics of the Bodhisattva

In Mahayana Buddhism, ethics is understood in a cosmic context. Actions have significance not just for the immediate present but for all beings. The bodhisattva doesn't practice ethics because he or she wants to feel better, but aims to serve the spiritual needs of all beings. Thus ethics becomes a direct outpouring of compassion. The bodhisattva recognizes that his or her wellbeing is intimately connected with the wellbeing of others and so his or her ethics expresses this solidarity with all life. Ethics becomes a spiritual service of the needs of all beings. In the words of the great poet-monk Shantideva:

I am medicine for the sick. May I be
both the doctor and their nurse, until
the sickness does not recur.

See, I give up without regret my
bodies, my pleasures, and my good
acquired in all three times, to
accomplish good for every being.[10]

Meditation

Meditation is widely seen as the signature Buddhist practice, yet it is not the primary focus of most Buddhists. In fact, many Buddhists don't meditate at all but rather prioritize devotional activities, especially giving. Importantly, meditation is not about making the mind go blank, nor is it even really about relaxing and relieving stress, rather it concerns cultivating and maintaining skilful mental states and ultimately seeing into the true nature of reality.

Buddhism encompasses a wide range of meditation techniques and approaches, and the purpose of any particular practice will differ according to the vision of spiritual life within which it is taught. A common distinction, however, is between calming meditation (*samatha*) and meditation that aims to contemplate and penetrate the nature of reality (*vipassana* or insight). More strictly, calming and insight are orientations towards meditation rather than categories of techniques. This distinction will serve as a starting point but we will see that some approaches to meditation do not fit neatly into either orientation but rather combine both.

In speaking of meditation, traditional Buddhism emphasizes four right efforts: preventing unskillful mental states from arising, eradicating unskilful mental states that have managed to infiltrate the mind, developing skilful mental states and maintaining them. This shows how there is an intimate connection between the practice of ethics and meditation. In meditation, we work more directly on the underlying attitudes that drive our behavior. The practice of meditation underlines how Buddhism functions as a kind of mind or attitude training because it sees mind as primary and as directing action. Moreover, mind is responsible for our happiness or distress and so through directly working on the mind itself we may enjoy more wholesome and satisfying experiences.

Samatha

Samatha means calm or tranquility and is regarded as an important dimension of meditation practice because it produces a stable, integrated state of mind which then permits the possibility of approaching the nature of reality more decisively, without distraction and without fragmentation. Mindfulness-based practices and the sublime abodes are often seen as promoting these qualities. Some of these techniques are outlined below.

MINDFULNESS

Mindfulness is a quality of awareness that enables us to be more fully present and aware in the moment. It is often associated with the cultivation of calm but it is also important in the development of insight. It allows us to identify more clearly what is happening in the mind, for instance: our mood, what thoughts are rushing past, whether we are angry, whether we are anxious, and so on. Through mindfulness, we may slowly peel away the layers that obscure our immediate experience and have a more direct contact with our sensations, emotions, and thoughts. This clarity about what is happening in our experience, and more specifically how we are constructing it in every moment, opens up the possibility of change. Through mindfulness, attention may be consciously directed towards more expansive and creative aspects of experience.

A classic mindfulness-based practice is known as the mindfulness of breathing. According to tradition, the Buddha attained awakening while practicing this technique which shows that it is not necessarily just about developing calm. In the mindfulness of breathing, the breath is used as an object of concentration to support the meditator in developing stillness of mind. Thought slows down, or even pauses, and the mind is relieved from its obsessive whirling, at least momentarily.

An early scripture speaks of four areas in which mindfulness may be cultivated. First, there is the body. This includes posture, such as awareness of whether we are seated, lying down, standing, or walking. It also includes awareness of the breath and even of the impermanent and constructed nature of the body. The second area is sensations. The meditator cultivates awareness of the sensations that arise in the body, more specifically, whether they are pleasant, painful, or neutral.

Third, awareness of the condition of the mind is cultivated, particularly of mood: whether one is concentrated or dispersed, happy or sad etc. Fourth, mindfulness is directed towards the contemplation of categories or lists that enable us to understand the nature of reality more clearly and accurately, such as the Four Noble Truths.

Mindfulness is also closely associated with the quality of ethical vigilance (*appamada*), the capacity to recognize whether we are in a skilful or unskilful mental state and the motivation to guard the mind so as to maintain ethical impulses and not feed unethical ones. A manifestation of this quality of ethical vigilance is a desire to protect the mind from unhealthy stimulus or 'guard the gates of the senses'. This involves recognizing how the mental states that we dwell in depend in part on the stimulation to which we expose the mind. If the mind is constantly overloaded with information or coarse stimulation, it is unlikely that when we meditate we will easily develop calm and tranquility. Consequently, it is important to reduce stimulation, and even block certain unhelpful input, if we are to refine our state of consciousness. Silence and doing nothing can be very fruitful in this respect.

Mindfulness is a quality that may be put at the service of aesthetic sensitivity too. We can see this in various Japanese art forms such as ink drawing. A master of the art may train for many years in order to produce a beautiful, simple image using just one brushstroke.

THE SUBLIME ABODES

The sublime abodes are a group of practices that encourage the development of ethical attitudes and motivations. Essentially, they are concerned with moving beyond an ego-cherishing attitude towards valuing others and being attentive and responsive to their needs. There are four practices in this group: the cultivation of universal loving-kindness (*metta*), the cultivation of sympathetic joy (*mudita*), the cultivation of compassion (*karuna*), and the cultivation of equanimity (*upekkha*). Metta is the root attitude and consists in a benevolent awareness or sensitivity towards all beings. It begins with oneself as one cultivates a generous, affirming, appreciative attitude towards oneself. This attitude is then extended to a good friend, a relative stranger or neutral person, someone with whom we have had a conflict (traditionally, an 'enemy'), and finally towards all beings. Metta is regarded as the ideal attitude and has no limits; it does not discriminate but is freely shared.

Sympathetic joy is the capacity to rejoice in the happiness and especially the virtue of others. Instead of falling into jealousy or resentment, which lead to suffering, sympathetic joy allows us to rejoice in the success and wellbeing of others. In this practice, one deliberately cultivates delight in the virtue and wellbeing of others.

In the cultivation of compassion, the meditator directs metta towards someone who is suffering and wishes that they may be freed from their suffering. In later stages of the practice, one contemplates with a heart full of metta that friends, acquaintances, and even enemies are subject to suffering. This encounter between loving-kindness and suffering inspires a compassionate response, a desire to alleviate the suffering of others.

In the cultivation of equanimity, the meditator reflects on both the joy and suffering that all beings experience and, through this contemplation, a loving and yet equanimous response emerges.

A samatha orientation towards practice may result in highly pleasurable and concentrated states of mind known as *jhana*. Instead of experiencing the mind as fragmented or dispersed, all of one's energies are in harmony and one is fully present in the moment. Traditional texts speak of a whole series of super-conscious states of ever-increasing subtlety and refinement. The enjoyment of such states of mind is seen as positive and desirable because jhana represents a state of increased integration, clarity, and positive emotion. However, the attainment of jhana is not the final objective of Buddhist meditation but rather permits the possibility of a sustained cultivation of insight, which in turn brings about a decisive transformation in the heart-mind.

Vipassana

Vipassana or insight does not so much refer to a specific technique but rather refers to an approach to meditation practices, particularly in terms of using these practices to grasp the nature of reality. For instance, through contemplating the impermanence of the breath, one may cultivate insight into the universal truth of impermanence. The sublime abodes too may serve as insight practices through contemplating universal truths such as the inevitability of suffering. Certain practices are more specifically designed to focus on such themes. For instance, a practice found in early Buddhism is the contemplation of the stages of decomposition of a corpse. While this might strike us as a bit gory and even depressing, it has the aim, first of all, to help loosen over-attachment to the body, to one's appearance, and sexual desire. Its deeper aim is to support reflection on impermanence, which results in a serene letting go.

While contemplating a corpse (either literally or through using the imagination) is a visceral way to connect with some difficult truths, other techniques are more conceptual such as contemplating the Four Noble Truths or the qualities of the enlightened state. One early Buddhist scripture presents a list of five things that we should constantly reflect upon. First, we may reflect that we are subject to illness, we cannot escape illness, and in fact all are subject to illness. Second, we reflect that we will grow old, we cannot hold back the tide of time, and all will age just as we inevitably must. Third, we reflect that we will die, we don't know exactly when but, just like everyone else, our final day will come. Fourth, we reflect that, sooner or late, and certainly at death, we will be separated from all that we cherish, all that is precious and valuable to us. We will inevitably have to let all of this go. Fifth, we reflect that we are the heirs to our previous actions, we cannot escape the impact of our actions, and our actions determine who we are. The purpose of such reflection is to inspire a renunciation of mundane goals and the aspiration to gain enlightenment.

A number of approaches to insight involve dissolving cherished concepts or ideas using a process of analysis, this is especially to help overcome the idea that anything has a fixed nature or identity. Visualization-type practices too may serve to deepen insight, in particular the visualization of enlightened figures which is described in more detail below. More will be said about insight in the following chapter.

Meditation in Tibetan Buddhism

Tibetan Buddhism has developed an intricate technology of meditation that is impossible to do justice to here. It incorporates a wide range of meditation practices often combined with ritual, chanting, and complex symbolism. To provide a taste of the rich array of techniques and approaches, I will summarize a set of practices known as the Foundation Meditations (*mula yogas*). These are: the going for refuge and prostration practice, the *bodhichitta* practice, the visualization of *Vajrasattva*, and the mandala offering practice.

The going for refuge and prostration practice has the aim of strengthening the volition to go for refuge to the Three Jewels. It does this through a complex visualization of a 'refuge tree', which appears in the midst of an infinite blue sky and is composed of pure light. It is populated by Buddhas, bodhisattvas, other deities and important historical Buddhist figures. The meditator then recites verses aloud connected with going for refuge and, while continuing to visualize and recite, performs a series of prostrations before the imagined refuge tree (traditionally 108). He or she imagines doing this alongside all sentient beings. The practice culminates in a process of purification by light emanating from the refuges. In order to 'complete' the practice, it is traditional to do 100,000 prostrations, which would take about two and a half years of daily practice.

In the bodhichitta practice (also known as *tonglen* – 'giving and receiving'), the aim is to develop and strengthen an altruistic orientation: to gain enlightenment not just for ourselves but also to help all beings towards enlightenment. Here one visualizes oneself in the midst of a scintillating blue sky. After calling upon the refuges, one cultivates an empathic attitude towards all beings and reflects that one's welfare is bound up with theirs. A verse such as the following may then be used for reflection:

All beings are essentially like myself
insofar as they desire happiness and
dislike suffering. All beings, myself
included, though desiring happiness,
do evil and therefore experience
suffering, again and again. Owing
to our own stupidity, like prisoners
unable to escape from jail, we all
revolve endlessly in samsara.

Reflecting on the futility of this situation, one resolves to guide beings away from suffering and to go for refuge to the Three Jewels more decisively in order to help others. One then recites over and over: 'With all beings, I go for refuge to the Three Jewels.' Whilst doing this, as one breathes out, one imagines that whatever skilful impulses are within begin to shine like moonlight and, with one's outbreath, that this light falls on all beings, entering their bodies and bringing them great bliss. As one breathes in, one imagines the unskilful actions of others, like a black shadow, leaving their bodies and entering one's own, where they are purified by the power of one's aspiration and converted into pure white light.

The visualization and mantra recitation of Vajrasattva (diamond being) is an example of what is sometimes called deity yoga, a practice central to Tibetan Buddhism, and in this case is particularly concerned with purification and confession. Deity yoga involves the visualization and ritual service of an enlightened figure who embodies wisdom and compassion. Through visualization, sacred verses, mantras, and even ritual gestures, the meditator aims to identify completely with the chosen deity, and so become a channel for the transmission of its enlightened qualities.

In the Vajrasattva practice, one visualizes the Buddha Vajrasattva, who appears like a young prince composed of brilliant white light and sits in meditation holding a golden *vajra* (a symbolic lightning bolt) in his right hand, which symbolizes reality, and in his left a silver bell. One recites a special mantra while pure white light begins to enter the body through the crown of the head purifying all evil and unskilfulness. This unskilfulness may be imagined as black sludge that is gradually cleansed. One then imagines all beings with Vajrasattva above their heads; each one being purified in just the same way. Once they are completely purified, and after reciting further verses, the visualization dissolves away.

The Mandala offering practice focuses on the cultivation of gratitude and generosity. It also concerns renunciation and the transference of merit: we want to share all the benefits we have gained from going for refuge to the Three Jewels with all beings, not holding anything back for ourselves. This practice is quite technical as it combines visualization, recitation, and a series of ritual actions. To do it, a mandala set (comprising a base, three rings, and a top ornament) is often used, but this may also be symbolized using a ritual gesture.

In this practice, the meditator constructs a symbolic universe by placing a concentric ring on the base and filling it with rice. This process is repeated until the top ornament is added creating what looks a bit like a small wedding cake. While doing this, the meditator visualizes the entire universe that he wishes to offer to the Buddhas and bodhisattvas and also recites verses of praise and gratitude. The mandala (or the universe) is then offered to the Buddha by tipping the whole assemblage into a carefully prepared cloth, and then the process may be repeated.

An additional practice that is sometimes added to this list is Guru Yoga. This involves the contemplation of one's immediate guru and of the lineage of gurus stretching back in time. The meditator asks for their blessings and is purified by them. The guru is regarded as the embodiment of the Buddha but, equally, so are all beings. In other words, Guru Yoga is a means to connect with the principle of enlightenment.

Puja, chanting, and mantras

Puja or devotion together with chanting sacred texts and mantras may also be regarded as meditation practices.

The purpose of puja is to cultivate and deepen faith in the Three Jewels, especially the Buddha. The meditator recites devotional verses, usually out loud and often in the context of a group, in order to cultivate an attitude of receptivity and appreciation towards ultimate values. There is a particular form of puja known as the Supreme Worship, which encourages the practitioner to adopt a series of ethical and devotional attitudes. One version of this practice is known as the 7-fold puja and has the more specific aim of cultivating the bodhichitta: a will or aspiration to seek enlightenment not just for oneself alone but for the benefit of all beings.

Chanting has been a key practice in Buddhism since the beginning. In an oral culture, it served as the main way to record, recollect, and transmit the teachings. In addition, it strengthens a sense of shared commitment and practice. Chanting a sacred text also permits the possibility of deeper reflection on that text. Certain texts have served as sources of unity for many centuries, such as the salutation to the Three Jewels in which one contemplates the qualities and virtues of the Buddha, Dharma, and sangha. Other texts, such as the *Heart Sutra*, may serve to prompt insight reflection. It is also true that chanting sacred texts serves as a kind of blessing and it has traditionally been believed that certain special texts have miraculous powers. Chanting them is believed to inspire changes in the world and to call forth blessings.

Mantras are strings of syllables, usually from Sanskrit, which have limited conceptual meaning. They serve as a kind of sonic meditation and are seen as invoking spiritual qualities such as wisdom and compassion. Many are directly linked to Buddha or bodhisattva figures, so through reciting the mantra one calls forth the qualities, and even the essence, of the enlightened being. Mantra recitation often forms part of deity yoga practice but may also function independently. Some Buddhist schools focus on mantra recitation or chanting as the key, even exclusive practice. For instance, in Nichiren Buddhism, an important school in Japan, the key practice is the recitation of the name of the *Lotus Sutra* (in Japanese, *nam myoho renge kyo*) as it is believed that all of the qualities of the scripture are concentrated in its name and so, by chanting it, the practitioner calls forth and absorbs all these qualities and virtues. In Pure Land Buddhism, also important in Japan, the essential practice is the mantra of Amitabha or Amida

Buddha (*namo amida butsu*), which essentially amounts to calling the name of this Buddha. In doing so, all of Amida's virtues and merits are transferred to the practitioner.

Formless practice

While a number of practices that have been described so far are quite technical and even complicated, there are other practices that have very little structure, sometimes referred to as formless practice. One example of such practices is *Dzogchen* (Great Perfection) found within Tibetan Buddhism.

The practice of Dzogchen rests on the idea of Buddha-nature, that deep down not only do we have the potential to become Buddhas but even that in some sense we already are. However, our true nature is obscured by our delusions, by our faults and failings. In Dzogchen practice, the aim is to dwell in awareness of this underlying, enlightened nature. Pristine awareness is what we ultimately are and have always been and our delusion is simply covering this up. We need to get back to our true nature. Such an approach to practice is optimistic because it underlines not our distance from enlightenment but rather our intimate connection with it. In addition, it emphasizes personal experience over conceptual knowledge or intellectual reflection. It is direct: something that can be seen in this very moment, seemingly it does not require decades of preparation. But it is also deceptive and elusive: the fact that we may conceptually understand that we are Buddhas deep down does not immediately result in the dissolving away of our delusions and distortions. This is still likely to take us a lifetime and beyond to work through.

Similar formless approaches are found in other traditions, notably zazen within the context of Zen Buddhism, as described in chapter 1.

Wisdom

The threefold way is not so much a series of consecutive steps as three elements or dimensions of the spiritual path that should be practiced simultaneously. Each informs and strengthens the others to form a kind of virtuous spiral. When speaking of wisdom in the context of Buddhist practice, it is important to keep in mind that it refers not merely to intellectual knowledge but rather to a kind of embodied wisdom that informs every aspect of body, speech, and mind. For this reason, we might see wisdom as having three aspects: a rational aspect which expresses itself in terms of clarity, an emotional aspect which expresses itself through confidence or faith, and a volitional aspect which expresses itself through action in terms of renunciation and compassion. In this chapter, we consider wisdom from each of these perspectives. Later in the chapter, we approach the elusive teaching of *shunyata* or emptiness and consider some Buddhist teachings about death.

According to one model, Buddhism speaks of three progressive levels of wisdom. The first is wisdom attained by 'hearing'. This is learning something for the first time; it could be through listening to a talk, studying a book, or even seeing a Buddhist quote on the Internet. At this level, we are simply learning, processing what we have heard in order to understand it on a basic level. The second level is 'reflecting' whereby we begin to think through the consequences and implications of what we have learned. We may also begin to apply it to our own experience. Finally, the third level of wisdom is 'meditating' or 'becoming', where we absorb what we have learned deeply into ourselves. It then begins to guide and influence how we live our lives without us necessarily even needing to think about it consciously.

To help understand the differences between these three levels, the analogy of learning to drive a car may help. The first level is listening to the guidance of our instructor; the second level is internalizing those instructions and following them in order to successfully negotiate the traffic; the third level is like driving spontaneously without even needing to think about how to drive, it is just now something that we can do, joyfully and safely.

1 Clarity: the three characteristics of existence

Buddhism commonly speaks of wisdom in terms of seeing things as they really are. While this metaphor has its limitations, it illustrates how the enlightened person relates to experience free of distorting prejudice; free of greed, hatred, and delusion which are the motors that drive the unenlightened mind and cloud our judgment, leading us to make decisions that aggravate our suffering rather than relieve it. In order to help us to see experience with greater clarity, Buddhism offers various conceptual models, one of the most important of which is the *three characteristics of existence*.

According to this formula, our unenlightened experience comprises three salient characteristics, which we should constantly reflect upon. First, our experience is unsatisfactory. Second, that experience is impermanent. Third, nothing within experience has a fixed, enduring essence. These three characteristics of existence do not aspire towards some essential, exhaustive description of the world but instead might be understood as three lenses through which we might contemplate experience. But why use these particular lenses? Contemplating each of these characteristics aims to provoke a transformation in our way of living, ultimately to open a door to liberation. They are not intellectual assertions which require assent but rather contemplative models that invite us to apply them and see where they take us.

UNSATISFACTORINESS OR DUKKHA

In considering the Four Noble Truths, we have already seen how Buddhism highlights suffering as a central aspect of human experience. Here the message seems to be that suffering is an inescapable, even integral part of being human. However, contemplating suffering as one of the three characteristics of existence is not intended to make us feel gloomy or depressed. Rather, the aim is to prompt us to look for something deeper, something more meaningful within life and to withdraw our investment in limited refuges or mundane pleasures.

Reflecting on unsatisfactoriness helps us to begin to see what is of real value in our lives.

IMPERMANENCE

Reflecting on impermanence has the aim of helping us to loosen attachment and accept the constant change that characterizes life. Instead of trying to resist change, which results in frustration and suffering, Buddhism encourages us to embrace it. While impermanence is often seen as a negative thing – our cherished cellphone will break or our relationship will end – it also has its positive side. Suffering is impermanent and can come to end. Owing to impermanence, we have the possibility of transforming our lives in all sorts of creative ways. Some Buddhist traditions, notably Zen, draw attention not only to the sadness that may accompany the inevitability of change, but also to the often exquisite beauty inherent in transience.

INSUBSTANTIALITY

The third characteristic of existence can prove more elusive and at first may seem a bit abstract. Buddhism teaches that nothing has an essence, or a fixed nature, that endures through time. In a way, it is a repetition of the idea of impermanence but has a slightly more philosophical flavor. The Buddha lived at a time when there was a widespread belief in the idea of a soul or *atman*. This idea was applied to the human being and it was believed that the soul transmigrated from body to body until it became liberated. While this may sound a bit like what we have already seen in Buddhism, it is in fact different. Buddhism teaches the idea of *conditionality*; one thing gives rise to another, rather than the idea of identity continuing through time. For instance, who

I am today depends upon who I was (and what I did) yesterday; there is a relationship of dependence but not of identity. A string of beads, for instance, are linked but there is not an essence that transfers from one bead to another. According to Buddhism, this reality applies to all things. Instead of seeing things as having an essence, Buddhism sees things in terms of conditioned arising: when the appropriate conditions are present, the consequent result follows. Conditionality invites us to recognize the relationships between things, how they depend upon one another, rather than seeing them as ultimately separate.

There are many teachings that aim to help us to see this truth but one of the most widely known is the teaching of the five *skandhas* which is concerned with helping us recognize that there is nothing fixed and unchanging within ourselves, that we are a set of processes. It is often interpreted to mean that there is no 'self' or 'ego'. This can be quite confusing because it appears to contradict our everyday experience but it aims at a deeper, philosophical truth. It is not that we are figments of our own imagination but rather that how we define ourselves to some extent distorts the conditioned, ever-changing, elusive nature of what we are.

The five *skandhas*, as applied to the human being are: form or the body, consciousness, sensations, perceptions, and volitional tendencies (*samskaras*). While this might even strike you as an odd way to divide up human experience, it is important to remember that the purpose of doing so is not to learn to see that we are 'really' made up of these five categories. The purpose is to dissolve away the persistent attachment to the idea that there is indeed anything about us that is fixed and unchanging, to help us to see that there is no ultimate self behind it all. This emphasis on having no fixed nature is intended to help us to let go of attachment to a certain idea of who we are and so open up to the ever-changing mystery that is our moment-to-moment experience.

2 Faith or confidence

Faith in Buddhism has already been touched on in chapter 1 but it may come as a surprise to see faith presented as an aspect of wisdom, even of enlightenment itself. In Buddhism, faith may be divided into various categories and levels, one of these might be described as assurance. This kind of faith is not an uncritical trusting in the unknown or unknowable but a serene confidence in our connection with the transcendent dimension of experience; a capacity to respond reverentially and to cherish what is of ultimate value. While Buddhism is sometimes interpreted as a somewhat rational tradition, this is far from the case. It is not that it is irrational but rather that it addresses and calls forth aspects of human existence that cannot be touched purely through reason.

A leading example of how faith may be seen as central to spiritual awakening may be found in Japanese Pure Land Buddhism. According to Shinran, a key teacher from this lineage, the object of practice is to attain faith or deep entrusting (*shinjin*) rather than to attain wisdom or knowledge. Effectively, in this system, faith *is* knowledge. Faith of this kind is not expressed through dogmatism or arrogant superiority but rather through *faithfulness*, continuity of purpose, humility and gratitude. It is trusting that we have been primordially gifted the *chintamani*, the gem that grants our deepest wish, which is to fulfill our potential for enlightenment. Deep entrusting involves letting go of the ego-cherishing tendency, the naïve conviction that we can be the authors of our own liberation. It involves recognizing that liberation becomes possible when we surrender the ego-cherishing tendency, when we abandon our attachment to our own spiritual capacities, our obsession with our own potential, and open ourselves to influences that seem to come from beyond.

3 Renunciation and compassion

Buddhist wisdom or spiritual insight is transformative knowledge that inspires not just a shift of intellectual perspective but a change in the way life is lived. Wisdom has an impact. This impact might be understood as transforming behavior in two seemingly contradictory ways. Much of Buddhist practice is concerned with stimulating a letting go of attachment to samsara, the world of pain, the messy existence that most of us are stumbling our way through. Buddhism has always emphasized the importance of renunciation and yet this emphasis might give the impression that the goal is to escape from the complications of human life, to float free of them, leaving everyone and everything else behind to sort out their own problems. If that were true, it would indicate that Buddhism is a very individualistic, even a self-centered, tradition that has no care for the needs and sufferings of others. Renunciation, at root, is the renunciation of habits and attitudes that bind and limit us, and that cause us suffering; it is not running away from the world. At the same time, it is true that certain situations and conditions may reinforce our damaging habit patterns and so it may be necessary to withdraw from them, at least temporarily. This is one of the reasons why Buddhism has generally encouraged a change of lifestyle if one is to really break free.

Besides emphasizing renunciation, which tends to encourage withdrawal from the world, Buddhism also emphasizes the importance of compassion, which calls us back into the messiness of life to answer the suffering cries of beings. Compassion is not feeling pity for others but grows from an insight into our shared world and our common nature. If we are suffering, we obviously want to alleviate that suffering. At the same time, if we are able to activate our imagination, specifically our capacity to empathize with others, this same desire to alleviate suffering is likely to extend to others. We want them also to be free of suffering, not just ourselves. Compassion is the urge to alleviate suffering whatever its cause and whoever is living it. This compassionate response can be understood in terms of the arising of the *bodhichitta*, a kind of suprapersonal will that may erupt through us and which aims to respond to the suffering world in practical ways.

Shunyata

Shunyata is an important concept in Tibetan Buddhism and other Mahayana traditions. It is usually translated as emptiness and sometimes even as 'nothingness', which may communicate a somewhat, well, *empty* feeling. It is widely misinterpreted to mean that nothing really exists, as though everything were somehow a figment of our imagination (including ourselves). Understood this way, shunyata may seem rather depressing, even nihilistic – before we thought there was a world but now, seemingly, there isn't one. But this interpretation is a complete distortion. Shunyata is really a restatement of the truths of early Buddhism, especially conditionality and insubstantiality. It is concerned with remedying the tendency to take conceptual constructs as mirrors of reality, as representing ultimate, discrete realities. Shunyata is concerned with helping us see that nothing has a reality or existence independently of other things but rather life is an interconnected web of conditions. Even this, of course, is just a conceptual construct. Ultimately, shunyata points towards the elusiveness of all experience, how it seems to evaporate like mist when you try to grasp it. Experience is inconceivable.

According to one model, there are four levels of shunyata (according to others there are up to 32!) that may serve to show how it functions within Buddhist contemplation. In this series of reflections, we contemplate first that samsara is empty of the qualities of nirvana. In other words, samsara is not satisfactory, does not give lasting happiness, cannot be relied upon, is a limited refuge, and so on. The aim of this reflection is to be mindful of the limitations of samsara and to inspire renunciation of our attachment to it. In the second reflection, we contemplate that nirvana is empty of the faults of samsara: it is not a source of unsatisfactoriness; it is a reliable refuge, and so on. This strengthens our faith and motivation to move towards enlightenment. It draws us forward. In the third reflection, we contemplate that the distinction between samsara and nirvana is in fact empty. This is where things get a bit confusing. What it means to say is that samsara and nirvana are really modes of our own mind. It is not that nirvana is some other world, like a wonderland, into which we can pass through some spiritual looking glass, rather it is just the same world that we have always experienced but without the distorting prejudices, the out-of-control desires, and the confusions that color our present experience. In the final reflection, we contemplate that shunyata is itself empty. In other words, shunyata is itself a conceptual construct, it is not a reality behind things but rather, the realization that things have no behind. Shunyata is not an object, not even a reality, it is simply another tool to help us to relate to reality in a more satisfactory way, to recognize and appreciate that lived experience is a mystery that can never be fully defined or pinned down. In turn, this understanding may lead to a sense of openness, of wonder, even to what some teachers call 'beginner's mind', in which everything is always new, always fresh, as if experienced for the first time rather than filtered through memory or catalogued using readymade concepts.

Shunyata is the essential teaching of a short but important scripture known as the *Heart Sutra*, which is widely chanted as a kind of summary of the Buddhist perspective on wisdom. The *Heart Sutra* is a confusing, even paradoxical text, not easy to engage with without significant background knowledge of Buddhism. It appears to negate all of the basic concepts of Buddhism – the Four Noble Truths, the five *skandhas*, even enlightenment itself. It claims that all of these concepts are *empty*. However, this is not to say that they are meaningless, rather it is to caution against using such concepts in an overly literal way, to remind us that such concepts are fingers pointing to the moon of enlightenment, they are not enlightenment itself. Any model only works up to a certain point. To return to a key metaphor of the Buddha: the teachings are a raft to carry us to the other shore of awakening, nothing more or less.

Teachings about death and rebirth

Just as many other religions do, Buddhism sees death and how we deal with it as a crucial working ground of spiritual practice. After all, it is the only thing we can really be sure of. However, according to traditional Buddhism, we do not just live once but rather are enmeshed in a continual cycle of birth, death, and rebirth: samsara. Rather than perpetuate this cycle, which may seem attractive to some at least at first glance, the Buddhist goal is in fact to get off this merry-go-round through breaking the cycle that leads to future rebirth. This is done through realizing Nirvana or enlightenment.

In many Buddhist traditions death is seen as a crucial moment in this process and offers unique possibilities for liberation. In Tibetan Buddhism, for instance, many practices are dedicated to preparing for death. Indeed, the whole of the spiritual life is seen as a kind of spiritual death, which in turns helps to prepare for physical death. This is because death is the ultimate renunciation. When we die, we can take nothing with us, we will be separated from all that we hold dear. While this may seem a bit depressing, reflecting on it is intended to help us reduce attachment and withdraw investment from what is ultimately not important. In turn, this helps us to reduce our suffering.

According to Tibetan Buddhism, there are a series of pivotal moments in the process of life and death that offer opportunities for liberation. These are called *bardos*. Both the moment of death and the state between death and rebirth, which according to tradition lasts 49 days, offer the possibility of awakening to the nature of reality. Important texts, such as the *Tibetan Book of the Dead*, offer detailed instructions as to how to use the bardo of death to realize enlightenment. It is common to read these instructions aloud to someone who has recently died in the belief that they can still hear and that it will help them overcome their fear and embrace the clear light of reality instead of rushing towards a new womb.

The *Tibetan Book of the Dead* describes how the bardo consciousness sees a series of visions, first of wrathful and then of peaceful deities, which offer the opportunity of liberation. However, these enlightened visions strike terror into the heart of the transmigrating consciousness which flees from them. The purpose of reading the text is to inspire confidence so that the dead person embraces these visions of enlightenment, embraces the clear light of reality, rather than running from them.

While perhaps many of the details found in manuals like the *Tibetan Book of the Dead* may seem a bit remote, written in a symbolic language we don't understand, their intention is to invite us not to fear death, but to understand how it can help us to value life. Every moment is, in fact, a bardo, which means that every moment offers the possibility of liberation. Thus the present moment is supremely valuable: it is the moment of awakening.

Conclusion

Buddhism Today

Over the past century, traditional Buddhism has been bombarded by an armada of political, cultural, and historical forces. This has led to the weakening, displacing, and, even destruction of many Buddhist institutions. The influence of Communism has been devastating. Buddhism was virtually wiped out in Russia and Mongolia, and severely weakened in China. The Chinese invasion of Tibet in the 1950s led to the large-scale destruction of Buddhist culture, as well as to the exile of prominent spiritual leaders across the globe. Little is known of the fate of Buddhism in North Korea. While

Buddhism remains a part of Japanese culture, its traditional schools are struggling to adapt to a rapidly changing, technological age.

The catastrophic demolition of Buddhist heritage was perhaps most violently illustrated by the cultural terrorism of the Taliban military government of Afghanistan when, in March 2001, soldiers blasted to dust two colossal standing Buddhas, which had been carved into cliffs near the town of Bamiyan some 1,500 years before.

But it is not all doom and gloom. In recent decades, Buddhism has become increasingly visible and accessible across the globe. While there are still some countries where it is not possible to study and practice Buddhism, in the majority of developed economies its teachings are readily available. It has even been claimed that Buddhism is the fastest growing religion in such countries and while it seems unlikely (Islam is growing at a faster rate), there is no doubt that many people living in developed economies are sympathetic to it, even where they don't necessarily consider themselves Buddhists. Whereas in some of its traditional strongholds – such as East Asia – Buddhism has been in decline for centuries, it is now finding a new voice in countries that have more traditionally been Christian-influenced. It is something of an irony that while Christianity is becoming the dominant religion in South Korea and increasingly influential in Japan, Buddhism is finding a ready hearing in Europe, the United States, Latin America, and beyond. It is perhaps a further irony that at least some Buddhists from these countries are helping to reintroduce Buddhism to Asian countries, notably India.

The Dhamma Revolution

An important cultural and religious current in northern India, since the 1950s, has been the renewed interest in Buddhism, particularly among some of the poorest and most deprived (communities previously dismissed as 'untouchable'). A renowned leader of many of these people (now known as *dalits*), Dr B.R. Ambedkar, concluded that while he and his people remained wedded to Hinduism they would always be oppressed owing the caste system in which they were at the bottom of the pile. While less known than his contemporary Gandhi, Ambedkar is arguably an even more important figure of 20th century India.

Ambedkar concluded that to reject caste decisively, and to lead a more dignified life, he and his followers would need to reject Hinduism. It is impossible to overstate how revolutionary this proposal was and how far-reaching its consequences. After much research, Ambedkar concluded that the appropriate way forward could be found through converting to Buddhism, combining an approach to social change and inner transformation to inspire the uplift of the tens of millions of impoverished Indians, trodden down by caste.

Consequently, in a momentous ceremony conducted in Nagpur in 1956, Ambedkar received the refuges and precepts and so formally converted to Buddhism. What followed was astonishing. Ambedkar oversaw the conversion of an estimated 400–500,000 of his followers to Buddhism that very same day. Millions more followed their example in the months and years that followed. Today there are more than 8 million Buddhists in India, the vast majority of whom are 'new Buddhists' who converted following the example of Dr Ambedkar and who are from his home state of Maharashtra.

Tragically, Ambedkar died six weeks after his own conversion. This left his followers not only in shock and grief but also without any real understanding of the spiritual tradition to which they had converted. To some extent this situation continues today although a number of groups have been active in spreading the Buddhist teachings among the new converts, an example of which is the Triratna Bauddha Mahasangha.

New Schools of Buddhism

For the first time in world history, the entire intellectual and spiritual heritage of Buddhism has become available for study, including the recovery of large volumes of material that had been lost or neglected for centuries. This increasing availability of diverse Buddhist ideas and practices has stimulated unprecedented adaptation, experimentation, and innovation. Alongside this, Buddhism has been molded as a conceptual and historical unity, which has helped to foster the idea of a global Buddhist community, prompted intra-faith dialogue between formerly disconnected traditions, and encouraged greater convergence with regard to core teachings and practices.

While traditional forms of Buddhism have been transplanted to new fields, most often through immigration or exile, there has also been an upsurge of new Buddhist groups and movements which take their inspiration from some traditional school or schools but aim to develop an approach that is suited to the needs and challenges of post-traditional life. Contemporary Buddhist movements tend to share a number of key features that differ from traditional Buddhism. These include: a syncretic approach to Buddhist heritage; a softening – and even dissolving – of the monk/lay split; the softening or dissolving of spiritual hierarchy; increased individualism; a higher status accorded to women; a stress on meditation; an emphasis on the psychological as opposed to the 'religious'; and social engagement.

One such example is the Triratna Buddhist Community – the sangha within which I practice – founded by an English Theravada monk, Sangharakshita, in 1960s London. Originally known as the Friends of the Western Buddhist Order, it has attempted to find ways of translating traditional Buddhist ideas and practices into forms that could be applied to the needs of a non-traditional society.

At its heart, Triratna has a non-monastic Order open to men and women equally. Having abandoned the traditional monk-lay structure, members are known simply as 'Dharma-farers' (m. Dharmachari, f. Dharmacharini) and make individual lifestyle choices that best express their commitment to the Three Jewels. While many of the core teachings of Triratna are drawn from Theravada Buddhism, these are framed within a Mahayana mythic story, that of the 1,000-armed Avalokiteshvara. Each member is regarded as a hand of Avalokiteshvara and the Order collectively is conceived as functioning as a bodhisattva. Triratna affirms the unity of Buddhism and encourages the broad-based study of traditional teachings, as well as wider cultural enquiry, as means to spiritual transformation. A guiding principle of the Triratna Buddhist Order and Community is that going for refuge is the primary act of a Buddhist (as opposed to any particular practice or lifestyle).

Soka Gakkai

For many Japanese, traditional Buddhist sects are increasingly redundant, their temples little more than museums whose main role is to perform funeral and memorial rites. A number of new religious movements (NRMs), with varying links to Buddhism, have sprung up to fill the apparent spiritual vacuum. Perhaps the most significant Buddhist-inspired NRM is Soka Gakkai ('Value Creation Society'). Founded in the 1930s, Soka Gakkai expanded rapidly after the Second World War and reached a peak of 8–10 million believers in the 1980s. It places great value on education, and has established a successful university and a vigorous peace movement. It has also been active in international welfare programmes, including refugee relief and environmental conservation. Originally associated with a monastic wing, Soka Gakkai is now an exclusively lay organization.

Soka Gakkai has established groups in nearly two hundred countries and teaches the exclusive reliance upon the saving power of the *Lotus Sutra* and therefore emphasizes the recitation of the name of that scripture (known as the *daimoku*). Soka Gakkai has received some notoriety owing to claims that followers are encouraged to chant for material things, such as a new job. But the truth is that this type of practice is nothing new; it has always been a feature of popular Buddhism.

Secular and post-Buddhism

Buddhism generally has a good press in the contemporary world, even if perceptions of it are often over-simplified. It seemingly evokes peace, calm, contentment, and an easy atmosphere of spirituality. Buddha heads, and other icons, are widely used as domestic ornaments, and Buddhist imagery and ideas are regarded as assets in selling consumer products. Tibetan monks have been used to sell washing powder, IT solutions, and even paper tissues. Buddhist terms like nirvana, karma, enlightenment, and Zen are now embedded in popular culture. While these examples represent a relatively low level of engagement, they underline a general acceptance that Buddhism is a good thing. According to one survey, two million French people declared that Buddhism was the religion they liked best.

In past centuries, Buddhism has been central to the spiritual life of many Asian countries and has bequeathed a lasting cultural legacy. But, in our global era, the vast majority of people are reluctant to swallow the entire package. Religious affiliation in general is on the decline in many post-traditional cultures, especially those where Buddhism has become attractive. A diffuse impact of Buddhist ideas, practices, and cultural forms therefore seems more probable; far more people are likely read a book by HH the Dalai Lama, perhaps even go and hear him speak, than would declare themselves to be Buddhists.

Rather than making exclusive commitments to Buddhist practice, contemporary Western people are more likely to be 'sympathizers'. They may read Buddhist texts, meditate, participate in online chatrooms, perhaps even attend a Buddhist group, but they may also take an interest in other religious traditions and value the insights of Western psychology, combining many influences to create their own personal spirituality, seemingly free of institutional contamination.

A notable trend in recent years has been to strip away elements of Buddhism deemed to be unnecessarily religious, and perhaps off-putting, and to present a selection of teachings and practices to more secular-oriented audiences. A leading example is the growth of secular mindfulness where this teaching has been shared as a technique to help reduce stress, to support pain management, and even to alleviate depression. When used in these contexts, there is no expectation that those exploring mindfulness will want to become Buddhists or even that they are interested in Buddhism. It is likely that such trends will continue as fewer and fewer people seem to be drawn to formal religious practice in our increasingly secular age.

While trends like secular mindfulness imply that many more people can benefit from Buddhist teachings and practices, it is also possible that something will be lost in translation. Many, perhaps most human beings, have a yearning for something beyond themselves, even something transcendent. If this need cannot be met through religion, through gods or through the archetypal imagination, we are left with politicians, sports stars, or even celebrities who cannot possibly bear the weight of our ideals. Who can know what the future will bring, but it seems to me that there will always be a need for teachings like Buddhism that present a vision of transcendence, a template for a meaningful human life, and the possibility of deep human connection based on shared values. There will always be a need for The Three Jewels.

Going deeper

This book has offered a brief sketch of some of the main teachings and practices found within the Buddhist tradition. While we have seen that there are many shared principles, there is also great diversity. Above all, Buddhism is something to be applied and practiced rather than studied from the comfort of an armchair. This is the only way to understand its true intentions. The motivated seeker who wants to go further has the opportunity to explore a broad range of possible approaches to practice and this may be both exciting and daunting at the same time.

How to decide?

There is no easy or simple answer to this question. It is certainly not a question of saying that one kind of Buddhism is 'better' than another. It may indeed come down to circumstances, personal temperament, even whatever temple happens to be nearest. Whichever path calls your attention it will be more meaningful to explore the Dharma within a living spiritual community, rather than simply to read about it at home, although of course this is likely to come with some challenges. Dealing with real people, as opposed to simply reading about ideals, always has its complications.

I wish you well on your path.

Endnotes

1   Patrul Rimpoche, *The Words of my Perfect Teacher*, Altamira Press, 1998, p.11.

2   For a translation see Birnbaum, Raoul. 2003. *The Healing Buddha*, Shambhala Publications (rev edn).

3   T.666. Translated by William H. Grosnick in Lopez, Donald S (ed.). 1995. *Buddhism in Practice*, Princeton University Press, 94–106.

4   See Waddell, Norman and Abe, Masao, *The Heart of Dogen's Shobogenzo*, SUNY 2002, p.61ff.

5   Waddell and Abe, *op.cit.* 96.

6   Paradise Lost, 4: v.18-22.

7   Geoffrey Bownas and Anthony Thwaite (trans. and eds). 1998. *The Penguin Book of Japanese Verse* (rev edn). London: Penguin, 111.

8   *Gateless Gate*, Case 21. See See Katsuki, Sekida. 2005. *Two Zen Classics: The Gateless Gate and the Blue Cliff Records*, Shambhala, Boston, 77-8.

9   V. 1-2 Trans. Sangharakshita, Windhorse, 2001, p.13.

10 Shantideva, *the Bodhicaryavatara*, chapter 3, verses 8 and 10. trans. Kate Crosby and Andrew Skilton, 1996, p.20

Glossary

Ambedkar, Dr B.R. (1891–1956) Important Indian leader of underprivileged people who converted to Buddhism in 1956 inspiring the 'new Buddhists' of India.

Amitabha 'Infinite Light', an archetypal Buddha central in Pure Land Buddhism, usually red or golden.

Arahant 'Worthy one': the ideal of early Buddhism. Someone who has broken free of their spiritual fetters and reached Nirvana.

Avalokiteshvara Important archetypal bodhisattva who symbolizes compassion. In one form he has 11 heads and 1,000 arms.

Bardo Literally 'between'; in Tibetan Buddhism it usually refers to the transition between death and rebirth (but also other transitional moments).

Bodhisattva Literally 'awakening being' but refers to the compassionate orientation towards awakening in order to benefit all beings. Sometimes refers to human beings and sometimes to archetypal figures who symbolize compassion and wisdom.

Bodhichitta A kind of compassionate, supra-personal will that may emerge within a Buddhist practitioner calling him or her to practice for the benefit of all beings.

Buddha, the Literally 'awakened one', refers to historical founder of Buddhism or sometimes an archetypal figure that symbolizes awakening.

Buddha-nature Important teaching that emphasizes our capacity to become Buddhas, even that intrinsically we already are Buddhas.

Dalai Lama The secular and spiritual leader of Tibet.

Deity Yoga An approach to meditation that involves the ritual service of an archetypal Buddha or bodhisattva.

Dharma Usually the teachings of Buddhism or the truth. Sometimes refers to Buddhist scriptures.

Dōgen (1200–53) Important figure in Japanese Zen. Associated with the practice of zazen (sitting meditation).

Dukkha Suffering or unsatifactoriness; key to the teaching of the Four Noble Truths.

Dzogchen A form of meditation practice in Tibetan Buddhism concerned with seeing the inherent Buddha-nature.

Going for Refuge A Buddhist goes for refuge to the Three Jewels, which means to increasingly place these values in the center of their lives.

Jhana A state of super-concentration in meditation.

Karma Literally 'action'; a concept in Buddhist ethics that helps to explain how unskilful actions lead to suffering and skilful ones lead to happiness.

Lojong 'Attitude training'; important tradition within Tibetan Buddhism concerned with transforming the mind using pithy instructions and reflections.

Mahayana 'Great Way' refers to a broad field of Buddhist schools that emphasize the bodhisattva ideal, including Pure Land and Zen.

Mandala Literally, circle; a symbolic representation of the universe.

Medicine Buddha Archetypal Buddha associated with healing, blue in color.

Mindfulness A key practice in Buddhism concerned with the cultivation of self-awareness, especially the capacity to recognize and discriminate between skilful and unskilful mental states.

Nichiren Buddhism A form of Japanese Buddhism that focuses on the *Lotus Scripture* and particularly the chanting of its name: *Nam myoho renge kyo*.

Nirvana Literally 'extinction'; the goal of Buddhism, especially early Buddhism, and refers to the extinguishing of greed, hatred, and delusion, the causes of all our suffering.

Other Power Refers to Amitabha and his capacity to help beings to move towards awakening.

Pali Canon An important collection of Buddhist scriptures that record some of the earliest teachings, including the teachings of the Buddha himself.

Puja Buddhist ritual and devotion.

Pure Land An ideal world or universe created by a Buddha, which offers perfect conditions in which to awaken.

Pure Land Buddhism An important tradition in East Asia which emphasizes devotion to the Buddha Amitabha and rebirth in his Pure Land.

Rebirth The Buddhist idea that when we die, another being will be reborn who will inherit our karmic legacy.

Samatha An orientation to meditation that promotes calm and concentration.

Samsara 'Faring on': refers to the nature of the unawakened mind and how it experiences the world. Also often refers to the endless process of birth, death, and rebirth which for Buddhists is the realm of suffering.

Sangha The spiritual community within Buddhism, especially those who have become awakened. Sometimes refers to the community of monks and nuns but may also refer to all Buddhists.

Shinjin 'True entrusting': In Pure Land Buddhism, shinjin represents the attitude of trusting in the compassionate vows of Amitabha.

Shinran (1173–1263) Important Japanese teacher in the Pure Land tradition.

Shunyata Literally emptiness. A term that attempts to point at the ungraspable, undefinable nature of all experience.

Siddhartha The personal name of the Buddha.

Skandhas Literally 'heaps'; a list of five categories uses to analyze the human being in order to realize that there is no fixed self: body, sensations, consciousness, perception, and habitual tendencies.

Skilful Means An important teaching that helps to explain the unity behind diverse Buddhist teachings.

Soka Gakkai 'Value Creation Society'; important new school of Japanese Buddhism, emphasizing the *Lotus Scripture*.

Stupa Architectural monument which symbolizes the Buddha and awakening, found in many Buddhist countries.

Sublime Abodes A series of meditations concerned with cultivating: loving-kindness (metta), sympathetic joy (mudita), compassion (karuna), and equanimity (upekkha).

Sutra General term for a Buddhist scripture.

Tantra See Vajrayana.

Theravada 'Doctrine of the elders', an ancient school of Buddhism that survives in southern Asian and emphasizes monasticism.

Three Jewels The Buddha, Dharma, and Sangha. The three primary values or principles in Buddhism.

Tibetan Book of the Dead An important text which offers guidance in relation to death and rebirth.

Triratna Buddhist Order A contemporary, ecumenical Buddhist school emphasizing the unity of Buddhism.

Tulku In Tibetan Buddhism (Vajrayana) refers to someone who is apparently a bodhisattva and who chooses to be reborn to help the world (the Dalai Lama is an example). Often a lineage over generations.

Vajrasattva 'Diamond being'; an archetypal Buddha found in Tibetan Buddhism.

Vajrayana (or Tantra) An approach to Buddhism found in Tibet, Mongolia and some other parts of Asia which emphasizes ritual, secret teachings, and deity worship.

Vipassana Insight; an approach to meditation concerned with seeing into the nature of reality.

Yamantaka 'Destroyer of Death'; a wrathful deity of Tibetan Buddhism.

Zazen Sitting meditation, especially in Japanese Soto Zen.

Zen (or Chan) An important tradition in East Asia, especially Japan, which emphasizes the immediacy of awakening within everyday experience.

First published in 2018 by New Holland Publishers
London • Sydney • Auckland

131–151 Great Titchfield Street, London WIW 5BB, United Kingdom
1/66 Gibbes Street, Chatswood, NSW 2067, Australia
5/39 Woodside Ave, Northcote, Auckland 0627, New Zealand

newhollandpublishers.com

A record of this book is held at the British Library and the
National Library of Australia.

ISBN 9781921024825

Group Managing Director: Fiona Schultz
Publisher: Monique Butterworth
Project Editor: Kaitlyn Smith
Designer: Sara Lindberg
Production Director: James Mills-Hicks
Printer: Times International Printing, Malaysia

10 9 8 7 6 5 4 3 2 1

Keep up with New Holland Publishers on Facebook
facebook.com/NewHollandPublishers